SINGLL

TAKEN

CURSED

SINGLE

TAKEN

CURSED

Nicki Bell

Editing, typesetting and ebook creation by Laura Kincaid,
Ten Thousand | Editing + Book Design
www.tenthousand.co.uk

Proofreading by Brooke Washburn-Hazelip

Cover design by MiblArt

To Jessica,
I hope you read this when you're older and decide
to stay with me forever

Prologue

I chose to write this book after being happily married for six years. Well, most days. On days when he doesn't put the empty cardboard roll from the toilet paper in the bin, I am not happy. Despite me placing the bin right beside the toilet to make it easier. Why do they do that? Anyway, I digress...

Please note, I am not married to *any* of the guys featured in these stories. I'm lucky I found someone who I didn't dislike after our first, second and tenth date. The fact I got knocked up after six weeks of dating may also have been a factor, but that's a story for a whole other book.

I started reflecting on all the shit – and somewhat bizarre – experiences I'd gone through during my single years. One date scarred me so badly, I stayed single – and celibate – for four years afterwards. And to date, I've only had four serious boyfriends, including my husband – no surprise given I'd endured Dante's seven circles of dating.

Is some of it extreme? Yes, trust me, I lived it. Does it sound unbelievable? Yes, but again, I lived it, so how do you think I feel? I have a six-year-old daughter and when the time comes for her to start dating – I've estimated this to be around thirty-one – then you better believe I'll let her read this book so she can prepare herself.

If you're single? Enjoy these stories because that's what I wrote them for. To help you feel better about the men

– or women – who don't call you back. They've done you a favour.

If you're taken? Revel in the fact you don't have to endure dating anymore and enjoy.

Cursed or something? Take comfort in knowing there are thousands out there – myself included – who can sympathise with your plight. And laugh a little at how shit my dating life used to be. I promise I won't hold it against you…

Tricky Vicky

The jobs I ended up with were always on a similar level to my dates: atrocious. My short stint as a removal manager didn't turn out any different. Be aware this story isn't so much about a date as it is a proposition.

January was a slow month in the removals business – people were too hungover and broke to move – so I took the opportunity to skive in the work van and make my way through the bag of chocolate coins Gran gave me every year in my Christmas box. The work phone rang, and I crammed one more coin into my mouth before answering.

'Yup?' I slurred, still chewing.

'Got a job for you,' John informed me.

I hated John. All the girls in the office did. He'd slept with one of them – she shall not be named – in the disabled toilets at the Christmas do three weeks before. Then he'd told the warehouse guys every sordid detail – and how he'd bought her a chippy after it before stuffing her into a taxi. He'd also congratulated himself on not giving her any money for it because his limit was 'one free ride a night'.

The gossip found its way back to us upstairs after a week, like a dirty game of telephone. All highly exaggerated and over the top, just like John.

'Right.' I swallowed and flicked a stray piece of chocolate from my work fleece before it melted in.

'I've sent a job through to your laptop – make sure you get it. The name is Vicky Miller,' he advised.

'Cheers.' Then I clicked off before I could say anything else.

After checking the laptop, I punched the listed postcode into the satnav and set off. I hoped to Christ it turned out to be an easy job I could spread out until finishing time.

Being the person who calculated how many boxes and vans rich people's belongings could fit into hadn't been my master plan. In my younger years, I'd wanted to be a fireman, but being scared shitless of heights and fire eliminated that career possibility. Fireman Sam had misled me all those Saturday mornings when he'd made it look easy getting a cat down from a tree and chasing after some sheep. What a halfwit I'd been.

The house I pulled up to was a mess. There were weeds giving birth to weeds and a yellow-stained mattress leaning up against the wall.

I banged on the door and prayed nobody would answer so I could go back to eating my chocolate coins until 5 p.m.

Nobody did. I knocked again and gave it another minute before I turned to head back through the jungle, but just as my hand lifted the gate latch, I heard a coarse, 'What d'ye want?'

No gold coins for me.

I plastered a smile on my face before spinning back around to find a middle-aged woman leaning against the peeling door frame. In contrast to her grey hair, her face looked like she'd gone face-first into a palette of blusher.

Surely she knew my reason for being here? 'I'm here to give you a quote for removal. You phoned in half an hour ago?'

Realisation dawned. 'Better come in,' she said, standing back to let me enter the dull hallway. I eyed the mattress again before going in and closing the door behind me.

'Didn't think you'd get out here today.' She walked me through to the kitchen. 'I need the kitchen packed up – drawers, food, the lot.'

Up close, her skin glowed red and her eyes looked like she'd been snorting something.

'I-I'll write that down,' I stuttered, noting it on my clipboard and averting my eyes.

This woman's housecoat (or dressing gown as it's known elsewhere) billowed open at the front, allowing me a full view of both nipples in quick succession. If she bent over, I'd see her in all her pasty glory.

'Thanks. You want a cup of tea?' she breathed, going over to the kettle to flip it on.

'Sure.' I counted the cupboards and drawers, opening a few to examine the contents before marking the details on my spreadsheet.

She moved away from the kettle and sidled up next to me. 'You take sugar?'

I calculated the boxes this one room would need. The faint smell of musk and sweat wafted up my nostrils as I pointed to each cupboard in turn to check my final tally.

'Two.' I hoped to Christ she wasn't going to hover over me the whole time. Nothing worse than folk blabbing on and asking if you were going anywhere on holiday, before telling you all about the one they'd booked a year in advance. Why did I care if they were planning to pay a visit to see Sticky Vicky while in Benidorm?

The kettle came to a boil, and she busied herself preparing the tea as I counted for a third time. Out came a nipple as she set the cup down on the worktop next to me. 'I can tell you like it sweet.'

Oh, for the love of Will Ferrell, I'd walked into a bad porno – and she was old enough to be my mum.

She followed up with, 'I'm Vicky by the way.'

Dread crawled up my spine. This Vicky had a sticky look about her. And greasy. Putrid even.

'Go up and check out the bedrooms first, then you can work your way down,' she said with a wink.

I nodded and gagged at the same time.

Ten minutes later, I'd analysed how many boxes would be required to house her mountains of dusty crap and trinkets, including elephant-shaped ashtrays and Victorian china dolls. The one room left was the master and then I could piss off.

Leaning over the bannister, I shouted in the direction of the living room, 'Just the main bedroom to go.'

She didn't respond over the sound of Jeremy Kyle, so I took that as permission.

The floorboards creaked as I shuffled to the last room and edged the door open.

Now I knew the reason for Vicky's red face when she answered the door.

On the bed, still vibrating, rested a giant flashing purple dildo. At least ten inches. Next to it lay a long string with balls on it. Anal beads.

One of my coins leaped up my oesophagus and into my mouth. I gulped it back. It didn't taste as nice going down a second time.

'Never mind the boxes – I could be doing with a good unwrapping,' a voice wheezed behind me.

How the hell did she get up the stairs without me hearing her?

She nodded at the stuff on the bed. 'Fancy finishing me off?' Did this woman have no shame?

'Eh no, sorry, hen – company policy and all that. I've got a boyfriend – his name's eh… Ralph.' I edged my way to the door, but she blocked me.

'He doesn't have to know.' She leaned over the bed and picked up the beads. They looked wet. And sticky.

My brain told my legs to get out of there. Who knew if the crazy bitch was planning to strangle me with those things and stick the vibrator in my mouth for a Facebook post?

I scampered for the door and walked backwards down the stairs, clinging to the bannister. Between the speed and panic, I almost went on my arse twice, but this wasn't the time for taking chances. My eyes needed to stay on her as she tottered after me.

'Look, I've another job to get to. I'm not interested,' I squealed, racing into the kitchen to grab my clipboard.

'You are so – don't act it.' She kept advancing and threw the beads around my neck as I gathered up my sheets of paper.

Time to make a break for it – this was definitely not worth the commission. 'I don't want to stick anything anywhere, alright?'

I made for the front door, smelling freedom.

'Your loss, you tight bitch,' she screamed after me into the open air.

'You can stick those balls up your arse,' I screamed back, catching myself as I tripped on a broken slab at the end of the path.

A woman pushing her kid in a buggy stopped dead across the street and looked at me. I stared her out and she walked on in a hurry.

After jumping into the van and locking the door, I phoned the office to say I was done for the day.

The next stop was the corner shop for an armful of chocolate coins and a bottle of Malibu. A couple leaving eyeballed me, and an old guy in the drink aisle kept stealing glances when he thought I wasn't looking.

I banged my shopping down at the till and started flicking through my purse for the right notes while the young girl rang it up. She was fighting to keep from laughing.

Did I still have chocolate on my face or something? 'What's so funny?' I demanded while a queue built up behind me.

'Nothing,' the girl tittered.

'Thought so,' I snapped, picking up my goods and turning to walk out.

'Nice necklace,' the cheeky cow cackled after me.

Necklace? I put a hand to my neck.

There dangled a sweaty, sticky chain of balls that smelled of peppermint lube.

I should have been a fireman.

The MLM Tool

I shuffled with a hunched back through the door after a twelve-hour shift on the hospital's neonatal unit – my fifth one in a row due to my colleague pulling a sickie. I knew for a fact said colleague had been out for brunch and drinks with her 'sweetheart' when she should have been spewing her load thanks to a 'terrible bug'. Cow.

Oh, and don't be thinking, *Wow, what an amazing human being she is for being able to do that kind of job.* I wasn't anyone important like a midwife or consultant – I was a low-paid reception/admin worker, although the NHS gave it the glamorous title of 'ward clerkess'.

When I'd taken the job, I'd figured it would entail sitting on my arse for twelve hours, three days a week. How naïve.

Instead, I became the resident jack-in-the-box, running from one ward to another, standing for half an hour at a time waiting outside rooms for some junior doctor so I could pass a message on. I'd been warned every message could be life-or-death important, so I spent most of my shift telling doctors their husbands or wives had left spaghetti in the microwave for them.

I checked the microwave. No one ever left me spaghetti. My mum hadn't even left me out a banana.

Although I felt exhausted after working 7 a.m. to 7 p.m. for five days straight, I knew I wouldn't be able to sleep. I'd be lying in the dark raging that my mum or dad hadn't even left me some dry pasta before they'd headed out.

Rather than being sensible and heading to bed, I clicked onto Facebook, scrolling through pictures of someone's cousin's baby shower, adverts for Land Rovers and people's recommendations for guttering. Even my social media knew I was a sad bastard with no life. No boyfriend, no baby, a car that might as well have been powered by a hairdryer and no house to buy guttering for.

I kept going till I stopped at a picture my best friend had commented on – a group of guys topless at a football park. I didn't recognise any of them. She'd written underneath it, *Looking good, boys.*

How original, Donna.

I couldn't help replying to her comment. *Could you sound any more like a pervert?*

She responded seconds later. *So?* Followed by a bunch of laughing emojis.

My phone pinged with a text.

It's my next-door neighbour and his pals. What'd u think?

About your originality when it comes to chat-up lines or the football park in the background? I think I can see a homeless guy on a swing.

Three dots for about five minutes.

No wonder you're single, Donna replied.

I laughed. *Touché.* I knew she wouldn't reply for another ten minutes because she would be googling what 'touché' meant.

Returning to Facebook, I spotted two notifications and clicked them open. Someone called Alan Davis had both liked and replied to the picture. I braced myself for either a slagging or a sleazy comment.

Not only had he liked my comment, but he'd also responded with, *Yeah, Donna, we're not just pieces of meat.* And just the one eye-rolling emoji.

I liked this guy's sarcasm.

A quick look at his profile picture made it easy for me to spot him in the group pic – tanned and with a body that told me he didn't spend every waking hour in the gym. Maybe because he had a demanding size-eight bird who wouldn't let him lift weights when he could be taking her picture in front of Selfridges for Instagram.

I hated those birds.

Alan Davis sent you a friend request.

I panicked. Why did this guy want to be my pal? He didn't know me. Maybe he hoped to trawl through my photo albums and find something incriminating? Like that one from Stacey's hen in Marbella where I'm deep throating a hot dog for a dare.

I panic-scrolled to the offending picture and deleted it.

Jesus Christ, just accept it. If he turns out to be a weirdo, you block him, I scolded myself.

Click. Done.

By the time I'd rummaged up something to eat – an apple and a packet of Hula Hoops – I had a private message from Alan.

Just wanted to say hi. And let you know I'm not a weirdo. In case you thought otherwise.

How did he know?

My fingers whizzed over the keys. *Not at all.*

Right away he wrote back. *I like connecting with new folk on this. What about you?*

I used Facebook to spy on everyone else's life and sometimes an ex. But I couldn't write that.

At a loss I settled for: *Aye, connecting is cool.*

Three dots appeared instantly. *I have this opportunity coming up with my job and I think you'd be great for it. If you're free tomorrow, do you fancy meeting up and I can talk you through it?*

I choked on my apple slice and threw the remainder onto the coffee table.

What kind of opportunity? I delayed opening the crisps until I could get a vague idea of what he meant. No sense choking to death over a Facebook message.

God, Donna would wet herself at that.

Three dots again as I eyed my crisps. *Working with people, a lot of money in it and you can work from home, or anywhere in the world. Interested?*

Interested in not having to do twelve-hour shifts? A lot of money? Being able to slob about in my pyjamas with *Pretty Little Liars* on? Duh.

Sounds good, I replied before he could change his mind and pick someone else who looked or sounded more professional.

After a lot of back and forth, we decided on a place and time: 1 p.m. the next day at DiMaggio's in Glasgow.

I was running ten minutes late, and a parking warden hovering as I reversed into a space on the main road only added to the stress. I waited until he marched away to stick a ticket on a nearby Honda before dashing through the rain to the restaurant.

Alan was chilling in a booth by the window when I walked in. He was just as tanned in real life, and he smelled *amazing* when he stood up and leaned in for a cuddle. It's what I imagined Thor would smell like. All man and... forest. Or maybe salted seawater? And some sweat.

A laptop sat open on the table in front of him. I thought he'd maybe been catching up on work or playing solitaire while he waited.

Our drinks arrived within minutes – a margarita for him and a lemonade for me. I forced my eyebrows not to raise when he took a sip without even stopping to remove the umbrella.

I followed his lead and took a huge gulp of my drink before explaining, 'Sorry I'm late. Parking.'

He used the umbrella to stir his cocktail, 'Don't worry about it. You look great.'

I smiled. 'Thanks. You too. I'm just glad you look like your profile picture. I couldn't have handled meeting a forty-year-old called Dave who ate Cornflakes for every meal.'

Even his laugh sounded gorgeous. 'Glad I met your expectations. So do you want to get started?'

'Sure, so what's this job you were talking about? Is it PR or something like that? I did go to college for marketing, but then I…'

He shook his head and I trailed off.

'I can show you what it is.' And with that, he turned his laptop around to face me, a video already queued up on the screen. 'It lasts about ten minutes and then I can go through all the details with you.'

I nodded, feeling lost. He hit the space bar for me and sat back in his seat, looking smug.

And then, I lost ten minutes of my life that I'll never be able to get back. It was a video of a bunch of random people talking about skincare products and how they'd changed their lives. They'd given up their nine-to-fives and were making twenty-five grand a month. A collage of pictures showed them standing in front of Mercs and Range Rovers with red bows on them – all because of this job. Apparently they holidayed in Dubai four times a year while making money. Passive income must have been mentioned 246 times.

An eternity later, the closing credits rolled. Alan shut the laptop lid and stared at me, waiting for a response.

What the fuck did any of that mean? That was the question running around my brain.

I gulped down the last of my lemonade to fill the now pulsating awkward silence, which I'd expected to be filled with him laughing – like this was his idea of a joke.

His eyes narrowed. 'So… what're your thoughts?'

My thoughts are that it's complete bullshit and anyone who believes it needs their head checked. Out loud, I said, 'It sounds eh… unrealistic. I mean twenty-five grand a month?'

He reached for my hand over the table. 'It's realistic. My upline is making over fifty a month. She just qualified for an all-expenses-paid trip to South Africa. You could as well – and you get a plus one.'

'So I could just be your plus one then?' I teased.

He didn't get it. 'You'd be a great addition to the team; you just need to sign up on the website, and I've brought a booklet for you.' He whipped a brightly coloured brochure out from under the table. 'Once you buy the starter kit then we can get you to start building a team of your own.'

'Team?' I snorted. 'Yeah, I don't think so.'

He didn't seem to hear me – or chose not to. 'The kit is £800, but you make over two grand once you sell everything.'

We needed a desperate change of subject to save this date. He was good-looking – like, out of my league, good-looking. I had to give him the benefit of the doubt. 'Thanks, but I'm not interested. Anyway, what do you fancy—'

He interrupted with more of the rehearsed spiel. 'And you can get your pals involved – the more people you recruit, the more money you make. Wouldn't you love to go on holiday whenever you felt like it? You can, thanks to Glory Skin.'

Glory Skin? That was the final straw. This guy wasn't interested in me. He just wanted to sign me up for some daft pyramid scheme that involved trying to sell face masks for £50 a time.

Everyone I knew had no money, including me. Time to cut my losses.

'Again, no thanks. I'm just going to go. Nice meeting you.'

I stood up, grabbing my jacket and bag. In normal circumstances, I'd have offered to pay for my drink, but I reasoned that he owed me for wasting thirty minutes of my time.

Alan looked panicked. 'Please don't go. I haven't even told you about the awards we've won for skincare. The moisturiser just glides on…' He made a grab for my arm, and I dodged it.

'If this is what you talk about with girls then I think you'll be needing that moisturiser more than anyone to amuse yourself at night,' I retorted.

'And Glory Skin is a shite name,' I shouted over the noise of the restaurant before storming out.

NoFap

My unfortunate episode with Mike occurred at my friend's daughter's christening. I turned out to be the one female there without a kid for a start, which meant I spent most of the day hanging around the bar, trying not to look like a sexual predator. And also to try to avoid the inevitable whining radiating from every child in the room.

I wanted kids one day, and I felt sure I would love them. But everyone else's just pissed me off. One brat decided to throw a strawberry at me in the church, leaving a stain on my new cream-and-navy midi dress.

Parents who fed their kids fruit that could potentially stain during religious ceremonies also pissed me off. I wanted to scream, 'Give the kids some Skips and stop trying to be pretentious.'

The minute a waiter announced the buffet was open, I hightailed it for the sausage rolls and pizza. I counted out five sausage rolls then threw an extra two on my plate, plus two slices of pizza.

'That's not all for you, is it?' a voice behind me queried.

Turning, I took in a blonde guy in a beige suit. No fruit stains in sight. His plate held two sandwiches, a pile of pakora and some salad.

'Yup, it's my one reason for coming to these things,' I responded, grabbing a bunch of napkins before exiting the queue and walking towards the bar.

The blonde guy trailed behind me. 'Where are you sitting?'

'Um, table two, but I've spent most of the day hiding out here,' I answered through a mouthful of sausage roll. The smell was too appetising for me to wait any longer.

'Bar it is then.' He smiled and pulled out a stool for me before taking one for himself. 'I'm Mike, by the way.'

I swallowed. 'Nicki. Nice to meet you.'

He picked through his salad. 'How do you know Lauren and David then?'

'Grew up with Lauren.' I took a bite of pizza and tried not to groan with satisfaction. This catering was worth looking like a paedophile for. 'You?'

He signalled the bartender, asked what I wanted to drink and ordered himself a whisky before turning back to me. 'I work with David. There's a few of us here, but they've all got their wives or girlfriends with them. I'm the odd man out.'

I nodded. 'Same here. And no kids. Do you…?'

Mike shook his head vigorously. 'Oh God no. Kids are just… God, I'd kill myself.'

OK… Bit of a strong statement.

He took my silence as a reason to carry on explaining. 'I mean, the only reason people should have sex is for an orgasm, right?'

A lump of margherita caught in my throat. 'Ummm…'

Mike picked up a pakora. 'I'll be honest, I had far too much sex over the years, but thank God I never knocked anyone up.'

I wished I hadn't been the first one at the buffet table.

The bartender placed a vodka and orange juice in front of me and I downed half of it. 'Yeah, thank God.'

He peeled the batter from the pakora yet didn't eat it, just threw the whole thing back onto his plate. 'I tried that NoFap, but it just made me raging *all* the time.'

This guy confused me. I'd never heard of a diet called NoFap, and I'd tried *all* of them. 'What's that?'

Mike's eyes lit up. 'It's this way of overcoming addiction to porn.' He stopped to take a bite of his ham sandwich. 'And masturbation. Meant to improve your health and life, and all that shit.'

Had I ended up sitting with a guy who talked about wanking with a stranger? Of course I had.

I mumbled, 'Sounds interesting,' and hoped to God he'd shut it.

He didn't.

He tore the remainder of his sandwich into pieces. 'They try to tell you to abstain for a week or a few days, but I ended up going mental at every little thing. I figured out that once every other day is best – means I get a good load and don't kick off.'

The sausage roll on a trajectory to my mouth never made it. It bounced off the bar and onto the floor.

'I have to go,' I cried, pushing my plate away. My stool crashed to the floor in my haste to stand up.

Mike moved to right it while I gulped the rest of my drink. 'Alright, well, cheers for talking to me.'

He stuck his hand out to shake mine and I stared at it like my eyes were made of UV light. It looked innocent enough, but all I could see was sperm wriggling around on his skin.

I took a step back. 'Sorry, I have to ask: did today happen to be... one of your' – I made finger quotes – 'days?'

The question didn't faze him. 'Yeah, this morning, but don't worry, I did it into a sock, so I didn't need to wash my hands.' His potentially semen-covered hand still dangled in the air, waiting for me to take it.

'Thank God you were behind me at the buffet,' I replied before bolting for the door.

I haven't been able to eat a sausage roll since.

Ba Ba Weird Sheep

My first and last foray into the dating-app world ended up being a belter, to say the least. Paul and I had spent a couple of weeks going back and forth on messages before arranging to meet at a bowling alley. I hated cinemas for first dates because it always felt like you were sitting in self-conscious silence – even though you were meant to be watching the film… in silence.

I arrived first and waited at the front door as planned. Torrential rain bucketed down, but I remained outside. I didn't want to take the chance of seeking shelter in the foyer and have him thinking I hadn't turned up.

They'd all be whispering, 'Aw, look at the saddo, bowling on her own. And she's shit at it as well – she keeps throwing the ball into the gutter.'

So I hopped from one foot to another and pulled my cardigan over my blow-dry in a vain attempt to keep it from being ruined.

Paul turned up fifteen minutes late, unconcerned with being late or soaked despite having a jacket with a hood.

I waved to get his attention from where I huddled under a canopy. 'Hi.'

He didn't say hi, hello or even good afternoon. Instead, he made a noise that I couldn't make out due to the thunder now roaring in the distance.

I gestured to the door then pulled it open. Once inside, I shrugged my cardigan back into its rightful place and shook my hair out.

A quick scan showed the place was heaving, despite it being a Thursday night.

'We should go and get our shoes,' I suggested, pointing over to the main desk.

Paul stared at me with a blank expression. 'Baaaa.'

Did he just make a… sheep noise? The amusements to the left of us were loud but I could've sworn that's what I'd heard.

I tried again, pointing to his jacket. 'You better take that off – you'll be roasting.'

'Baaa,' he bleated.

'OK, I get it, you're funny. Let's go.' And I stalked over to the main desk and requested my shoe size.

Paul followed but stood a few inches over to my left as if he wasn't with me. I was curious as to how he would communicate his shoe size in sheep language.

The red-faced teenager threw my shoes onto the counter and turned to him. 'Size?'

Again, Paul responded with a series of bleats.

The teenager looked at me. 'Is he with you?'

What else could I do but nod? However, I wasn't going to admit we were on a date.

The teenager pursed his lips and leaned over the counter. 'Is he no' right or something?' he whispered behind his hand to me.

The guy was pretending to be a fucking sheep on a first date so I was pretty sure he was 'something'.

I shrugged, and he turned towards the shoe compartments. 'Tell you what, mate – I'll point to the numbers, and you let me know when I come to your size, alright?'

He started at eight and worked his way upwards. When he came to the size elevens, Paul gave a loud, 'BAAAA.'

A family of four returning their shoes gave us a weird look before hurrying away when they caught my eye.

Take me with you, I wanted to shout after them. *Don't leave me here with Lambchop.*

A twenty-something female colleague of the teenager turned up and asked how many games we wanted. I told her one. I couldn't face any more than that.

Paul pulled a wad of notes out of his wallet and bashed them on the counter. He might've thought he was a sheep, but at least he acted like a gentleman. Or gentlesheep.

The girl counted out the correct number of notes, placed his change and receipt in front of him and instructed us to head to lane four. With grubby hands, he pocketed it all and lifted his shoes.

When we reached lane four, my heart sank – we were smack bang in the middle of the place. Which meant everyone could see us and hear Paul. I sat down and changed my shoes (they were weirdly trusting here, letting us keep our own shoes rather than holding them hostage behind the counter; either that or they didn't much care if people nicked stuff), praying no one I'd ever met in my life frequented the place.

Bending over to tie the faded red-and-blue laces, I noticed Paul's choice of footwear: flip-flops.

Flip-flops? In October. In Scotland. On a first date. To go bowling, where you were required to wear shoes worn by hundreds of others before you. A hotbed for all manner of foot diseases.

The baa-ing had distracted me to the point I hadn't taken in his whole attire. He'd slid his flip-flops off, tugged the shoes on and was now starting to remove his jacket.

I regretted telling him to take it off. Underneath was a canary-yellow shirt with rainbow braces. I wanted him to put it back on – I didn't care if he passed out with the heat.

A glance around told me other bowlers hadn't noticed the Pee-wee Herman impersonator in their midst. Yet.

I took a seat at the table and typed in our initials, my fantasy of thinking up cute nicknames for each other to display on the screen long gone.

'You're up,' I told him and took a seat.

'Baa, baa.' He smiled at me and walked over to pick up a ball. I took that to mean *thank you*.

With great concentration, he took a run towards the lane, stopping just shy of the line, and hurled the huge green ball he'd picked. I calculated it weighed more than him.

It careered down the middle before rolling over into the left-hand gutter.

He threw his hands up in the air and shrugged at me before sitting down again. I took that to mean 'I'm not bothered'.

Now my turn. I picked a lightweight pink ball in the hopes that I could throw it further and get a strike for the first time in my life.

My hopes were dashed after 0.2 seconds when my ball followed Paul's into the gutter.

No sympathetic look from him – instead, just a long, hard stare. Like the kind I imagined serial killers give you when they're trying to decide whether to stab or choke you.

He retrieved his green monstrosity of a ball, body bent forward with the weight.

With all the force he possessed, he launched it with his right arm, causing one of his braces to break free of his trousers. Not jeans but proper dress trousers. The kind my grandad would wear to weddings. In the fifties.

I waited for the thing to roll into the gutter so I could take my turn. Five more shots each and I could get out of here.

The green monstrosity defied all odds and continued on a straight path down the middle of the lane at lightning speed, taking out every pin. Holy shit, the sheep had pulled off a strike.

Paul flung his arms in the air before turning around to face me. 'BAAAAAA.' No longer a soft bleat, it could be heard around the alley and over the bleeping of the amusements.

He snapped off his other brace and yanked his trousers down, revealing boxers covered in what looked like hand-drawn sheep in felt tip. 'BAAAAAAAAAA,' he drawled again, punching the air in victory.

Everyone in the place gawked, and after hearing what they must have presumed to be an escaped farm animal, the teenager and three other members of staff appeared.

I took this as my cue to leave. Paul was about to be arrested for indecent exposure and impersonating a farm animal – if that was indeed a thing.

I lifted my jacket and bag, then crept back through the crowd gathered around our lane. I made a run for the exit as soon as I'd escaped them.

When I got home and went to change, I saw my feet, still clad in the bowling shoes.

Thanks to Paul, I lost a pair of £120 Nike trainers. And the ability to eat lamb.

No Dealer

The 'scariest' date I've ever been on occurred when I was a mere twenty years old. I'd ended up one of the few in my group of friends who hadn't headed to university after finishing high school. Not because I didn't get in. No, no, I decided in my teenage wisdom that I wanted to be making money right away instead of being stuck in a lecture hall. So I did, by continuing to work the breakfast shift at McDonald's. Making the same money I'd been making since my first shift at sixteen.

Clever, right?

Thanks to my idiotic decision, I lived vicariously through my friends and their student lives – which revolved around the student union.

One of my guy friends invited a bunch of us to his union one Thursday night, where it was BOGOF on any drink. Cue a train into town at 5 p.m. to take full advantage of it. David then snuck us in, and for two hours I revelled in double helpings of vodka and Irn-Bru. When a random guy with a cast on his arm joined our table, I didn't take much notice to start with, until David elbowed me in the side.

'Ow,' I shrieked, almost dropping my free drink.

David shouted into my ear over the music. 'That's my pal Andy,' he explained, gesturing to him.

I eyed him. His hair hung a bit too long, and he wore a T-shirt that appeared two sizes too small. From my seat, his nipples looked bigger than mine.

'Cool,' I answered – and went back to swaying to the music.

David wasn't giving up. 'I talked about you then showed him your picture,' he went on.

That got my attention. 'What picture?' I grabbed his elbow. 'Not the one from Kyle's eighteenth?'

He removed my hand and patted it. 'No, your profile picture on Bebo.'

Aw, thank God. He'd seen the one where my teeth didn't look squinty, my hair billowing after a fresh cut. Not the one of me sitting on the pavement with an eyelash stuck to my nose.

David downed the last of his pint. 'Want me to introduce you before I go to the bar?'

I gave him a wide grin. 'Why not?' If he turned out to be my soulmate, I could take all his T-shirts and wear them instead of him. Since he must have been buying them in my size and not his own.

David stood up and indicated to Andy that he should take the seat next to me. After a bit of shuffling, we were face to face.

'Hi.' He smiled and stuck out his free hand. 'Andy. Student.'

I gave it a cursory shake. 'Nicki. Minimum-wage worker selling hamburgers.'

He looked impressed. 'I like hamburgers.'

I nodded. 'I like when I don't smell like them. What's the deal with the cast?'

My question surprised him. 'Eh, I broke it at work. Can't get it off for another two weeks.'

'That's crap,' I said, feeling a bit sorry for him. 'What do you work as?'

It took him so long to answer I wondered if he'd heard the question. 'I have my own business for deliveries… and stuff. Started about a year ago and it's doing well. Managed to buy a flat six months ago.'

Impressive. I'd never met an entrepreneur before – or anyone who'd bought a house at my age. I couldn't afford a Care Bear to add to the collection in my bedroom.

'That's amazing,' I said. 'You must have a good work ethic.'

He looked satisfied at that statement. 'Well I didn't have a choice – my mum put me in foster care when I turned ten because I kept setting fire to stuff in the house. She bought me this revolting wooden bed – remember that pine that was all the rage in the nineties? My mum decorated my entire room with it – drawers, wardrobes, the lot. And I hated it, so I'd start a fire to burn it. When I almost torched the house by accident, she couldn't handle it.'

This was who David had set me up with? A pyromaniac? No wonder he'd fucked off to the bar and had yet to return.

I pretended to fumble in my bag. 'Well, it's good you got better.' My fingers grasped a lip gloss, and I took my time applying it, praying he didn't think a kiss would be following.

Andy started shredding a beer mat into pieces, a skill with just one hand. 'Yeah, I went home at eighteen and applied here for the mechanic's course. It's worked out pretty well because I bought an Audi, so I'll be able to fix it if anything goes wrong.'

I elbowed him in the ribs. 'An Audi and your own house? That's some business! How do I apply for a job?' I meant it as a joke of course. I'd never be able to work in an office with this guy. What if he set it on fire because he didn't like the filing cabinets?

He started shifting around in his seat. 'Look, I know I've just met you, but you're easy to talk to, and I feel shit having to lie.'

Confused, I set my drink down. 'You didn't set fire to your house?'

Andy shook his head. 'Nah, I did that. I mean about the other stuff, like how I broke my arm.'

He'd lost me.

'How'd it happen then? Gymnastics?' I snorted with laughter and hoped the music had hidden it.

He looked me dead in the eye. 'Running away from the police. I jumped over a church fence and landed right on it. Managed to get away though. Fuckin' scum.'

My heart galloped. 'Why were you running?' This conversation didn't seem like it had a happy ending.

'Look, I do have a delivery business, but it's coke I deliver. I met some guys to do a deal and these pricks in a squad car turned up and started chasing me.' He scrunched his empty plastic pint glass into a ball.

Yep, worse than I thought.

'My dad's a cop,' I snarled.

Andy ignored my tone and picked up another beer mat. 'No luck.'

My jaw tightened. 'I think you mean *no luck for you*. Enjoy your night.'

News of my departure got his attention. 'You're going? Gimme your number and we can meet up next week or something. Could maybe book a suite at the Radisson and make a night of it?'

'You must be high on your own supply to believe that is *ever* going to happen,' I retorted. 'I have standards.'

That pissed him off. 'Yeah? What standard's that then… being a stuck-up bitch?'

The insult didn't faze me – I'd been called worse by parents buying Happy Meals on a Saturday morning. One even threw a cheeseburger with extra pickles in my face.

Out the corner of my eye, I spotted David weaving his way through the crowd to our table. 'My standard's simple – I don't date coke dealers, hash dealers, even antique dealers.'

That shut him up. He stood up and disappeared in the direction of the toilets. Perhaps to do some business.

I grabbed David before he could sit down. 'You're coming with me.'

'Where? What about Andy?' David plonked his two pints on the table and looked around for his pal.

'You're putting me in a taxi home – and paying for it – to make sure your pal Pablo Escobar doesn't follow me,' I demanded as I manhandled him to the exit.

A month later, El Chapo Jr got arrested after one of his afternoon classes. Turned out he'd sold a bag to an undercover cop outside the halls of residence.

The Bathmat

The summer I turned nineteen, I had what us Scottish people call an 'empty'. Translation – your parents were stupid enough to leave you alone in the house for a period of time. This would then entail friends spewing Apple Sourz down the stair carpet and trying to make your cat eat a teabag.

My 'empty' spanned an entire week thanks to a last-minute deal to Benidorm that my parents couldn't turn down – £500 for the both of them with all-inclusive thrown in. Good old Teletext. If you're too young to know what that is then google it. Those were simpler times.

I'd booked the week off work and planned to spend it lounging around and blasting Britney Spears without being interrupted by, 'Turn that boom-boom shite down!' from the living room below.

By that point, I'd been on three dates with Steven – a new start at work (still McDonald's) who covered the drive-thru.

When I first met him in the crew room, well, I couldn't miss him. No one could. He was six foot five and two feet wide. He had to hunch down at the drive-thru counter to be heard.

After four days spent in jammies and indeed listening to Britney's album on a loop (if you're too young to remember Britney in her heyday then I feel sorry for you), I spent two hours preparing myself for Steven coming over that Friday night.

And by preparing, I mean I changed into clothes that semi-matched with some clear mascara. We didn't have the Kardashians back then, or Instagram, so no one bothered as much with their looks. We didn't have iPhones to preserve our non-contoured moments. Most of my make-up came from the front of a magazine titled *Mizz*. It was a less narcissistic time – I miss it.

Steven had offered to bring a Chinese, and he arrived bang on 6 p.m. Steven was the most down-to-earth guy I'd dated in a while. You know what I'm talking about; you've read some of the stories by this point. He gave me compliments, turned up when he said he would and didn't appear to have any relationship baggage.

'What'd you get?' I asked as I walked through to the kitchen and started to empty the carrier bag he'd handed me.

He leaned against the counter. 'Kung Pao chicken. Never had it before – thought it'd be nice to try something new. Push the boat out.'

I pulled two plates from the cupboard. 'Well, you're more adventurous than me then. Chicken fried rice and chips is all I ever order.'

Steven lifted the container with his food and dumped it out on his plate. 'You don't get bored eating the same thing every time?'

I handed him a fork from the drawer and continued to plate mine. 'Nope. I like to know what I'm getting. I like my Chinese like my men. Predictable.'

That made him smile before he leaned in for a kiss. 'I'd like to think I give you a bit more excitement than a Chinese.'

I pulled away. 'Maybe. Let's get this eaten before it goes cold.'

I grabbed the bag of chips and walked through to the living room. I'd set up the pre-agreed *The Breakfast Club* to watch on DVD before he'd arrived.

We demolished the food in ten minutes and the first hour of the film remained uneventful. Steven and I hadn't progressed past the cuddling and kissing stage. Fine by me since my shyness and virginity stopped me from going any further.

Steven started to squirm on the couch. I put it down to 'frustration' and pretended not to notice. After another ten minutes of wriggling, he asked, 'Eh, where's your toilet?'

'Upstairs to the left.' I leaned forward to grab my glass from the coffee table.

He jumped up. 'Be right back.'

I paused the film, predicting that he would indeed be right back.

Ten minutes passed. I cleared the dishes away to pass the time. Another five minutes went by, and I pulled out the hoover to remove the collection of rice I'd spilled on the carpet.

I called upstairs, 'Are you alright?'

A faint voice called back, 'Yeah… just be a minute.'

'OK,' I shouted and headed back to the kitchen. I decided to wash the dishes in the hopes he'd be back by the time I'd finished. But even after drying them and putting them away, he remained indisposed.

Paranoia started to set in. The toilet was on the second floor, but surely he wouldn't have jumped out the window. If I went up there, would I find an open window and Steven with a broken leg on the decking below? How would he explain that? 'Oh yeah, um, I'd rather fall and break my neck than tolerate you for another minute.'

The clock microwave showed he'd now been up there for thirty-five minutes. I knew men could take forever to push out a shit, but c'mon.

I marched upstairs and tapped on the door. 'Starting to get worried now,' I called in a fake jovial tone – and not a panicked *why are you leaving me?* voice.

No answer, just a series of grunts, followed by a tap running. Then another groan emerged. 'Nicki, listen, my IBS is playing up. Can you get me a binbag?'

I suffered from IBS myself so I could sympathise. My flare-ups could last for hours, during which I'd be on the toilet and throwing up into a bowl at the same time to relieve the stomach cramping. Mum had given me my own designated sick bowl, which she'd housed in the cabinet under the sink after I'd spewed over a fancy guest towel.

I hesitated. 'Ugh. I know the feeling, but there's a bowl in there you can use if you need to be sick.'

Another grunt. 'It's not to be sick in. It's for… your' – a squeezing noise – 'your bathmat. I'm so, so sorry.'

That threw me. 'The bathmat? Look if you got some sick on it, I'll shove it in the washing machine, don't worry.'

'You won't be able to – you'll need to throw it out. I'll buy you a new one,' he pleaded.

'Steven, it's fine – everybody gets sick. I'll just rinse it in the bath before washing it,' I called back, congratulating myself on being such an understanding date.

'It's not sick. It's… I didn't make it to the toilet in time. I ended up on the floor and it just happened…' he whimpered.

He didn't mean… he couldn't mean… could he? Had he *shat* on my bathmat?

'Right, I'll just go get the binbag then,' I squeaked and ran downstairs.

Steven was right – I had to throw it out. Mum had kicked off when I'd got a dribble of vomit on that lilac guest towel. A bathmat covered in my date's diarrhoea would not amuse her.

I pulled a binbag from the roll under the sink then returned to the toilet door and gave it a light knock. 'I'm just going to leave it at the door. Take your time and come down when you're ready.' Then I remembered. 'Just leave the bag at the back door and I'll put it outside.'

I heard what sounded like a weak, 'Thanks,' so I bolted back to the safety of the living room to wait it out. I played the rest of the film, but I couldn't concentrate. All I kept thinking was, *I hope he hasn't used the face cloths to wipe his arse with.*

The toilet flushing and heavy footsteps alerted me to his impending arrival. I righted myself on the couch, trying to plaster on an understanding and not-at-all-disgusted face.

Steven poked his head around the living-room door and kept his eyes down. 'I, uh, put it where you told me. Again, I'm so sorry.'

I walked to the door and pulled it open to reveal him almost bent double. I guessed his stomach would be tender after all its excitement.

'It happens,' I tried to console him. Not to me, or anyone else I knew. But I didn't see any reason to kick the guy when he was down. Or lying down. After defecating on my mum's cream Next bathmat.

'Are you alright to drive home?' I asked, worried he might explode on the way and ruin his car interior.

He nodded. 'Yeah, I don't think I've got anything left in me.' What a pleasant image. 'It must have been the food that set it off. I won't be ordering that again.'

I located the key to unlock the front door. 'No more Chinese for a while.' I forced a laugh.

He hovered for a minute before stepping outside. 'You won't tell anyone, will you? Not that I think you would, but just… you know what folk are like. I'd never hear the end of it.'

I wanted to forget tonight's events even more than he did. I wasn't even sure I'd be able to have a bath up there ever again.

'Never happened.' I held my breath and gave him a quick cuddle. 'I'm back at work next week so I'll see you then.'

That appeased him. 'You're brilliant.' And with that, he hobbled out to his car.

'Hope you feel better,' I shouted before slamming the front door shut and locking it.

Now to deal with… the bag. Steven had had the good sense to double knot it, and I held my breath the entire distance from the back door to the wheelie bin, not stopping to inhale until I made it back to the kitchen.

'Another one bites the dust,' I sighed, washing my hands three times before heading up to bed.

The next day, I headed to the supermarket to replenish all the food and supplies I'd used before my parents returned on Monday. When I pulled back into the driveway and went to open the front door so I could bring the bags in more easily, I stopped dead as soon as my foot touched the path – a sparkling white bathmat lay on our top step.

I had to hand it to Steven – he could laugh at himself, and he could make me laugh. Because of that ingenuity, we ended up dating for six months afterwards.

After all, we all shit, right?

The Prison Guard

I met Liam at the age of twenty-four, on the second-last night of a girls' holiday to Gran Canaria. There were four of us sharing a one-bedroom apartment on the beach, so we'd all agreed not to bring anyone back. Not that I would have anyway – the single souvenir I wanted to bring back was a fridge magnet for my mum, not an STD.

Our favourite pub for the entire holiday ended up being a Scottish bar called Craig's. They played 'Loch Lomond' every night at closing time, and despite hearing it twelve nights in a row, it still made me sentimental.

That night, I cried as I finished my drink, not caring who witnessed my rare moment of emotion. The other three left to go to the toilet, leaving me on bag duty.

A huge hand tapped my shoulder from behind. 'You alright?'

I twisted around, taking in a huge hand, attached to a huge arm, which led to a huge body. He looked like he ate Highland cows for breakfast. The fluorescent lights illuminated the blood flowing through his sallow-skinned biceps.

I wiped my eyes and hoped that my pal Tina's waterproof mascara had stayed put this time. 'Me? Yeah, fine – just that song. I'm used to hearing it at weddings, or New Year's, not in places like this.'

He smiled. Even his teeth were huge. 'You cry at those as well? Or just on holiday?'

I could hear the girls returning, Anna still droning on about a PR guy for a nightclub we'd met earlier. He'd given us free passes for their foam party and now she proclaimed to be in love.

I didn't care if she gave birth to his son and heir, but no way could she convince me to walk into a foam party. Girls' holiday or not. Those events were consigned to my days as a sixteen-year-old and 'nipping' a guy in the middle of all the foam with your pals watching, while you swatted away wandering fingers trying to poke you in the wrong places.

I laughed. 'Just on holiday. Wait, you're Scottish.' We were in a Scottish bar, he talked with a heavy Scottish accent and, to top it all off, his brick frame wore a Scottish rugby shirt. Don't ask why that surprised me. I'm a moron.

He chuckled. 'Ah, what gave it away?'

I couldn't quite place his accent after two jugs of Sex on the Beach. I felt the girls watching me as they retrieved their bags. This was the first guy I'd held a conversation with the entire time we'd been here. Everyone else had always ended up being too drunk, too coked out of their face or too 'handsy'.

'We'll get you outside,' Tina told me and gave him a cursory smile. When they were behind him, she mouthed, 'Nice,' and all three of them started gyrating. My friends, ladies and gentlemen – the height of maturity.

'Psychic,' I quipped.

We spent a brief couple of minutes on small talk – I discovered he came from Edinburgh – and he asked if we'd be back the next night. I told him yes – unless Anna tried to pull us into the sex-dungeon place like she'd attempted earlier on. 'For a laugh,' she'd tried to persuade us. Sure, Anna – whatever you say.

So we arranged to see each other the next night. Turned out he'd been here for a week already – with three friends as well – and still had a week to go. Lucky bastard.

The next morning at the pool, I'd been flippant when I told the girls about our quadruple date. All talk of sex dungeons and foam parties got thrown to the side. They sniggered and dreamed, hoping Liam's friends turned out to be as gorgeous as him. I hadn't managed to get a look at them the night before – Liam explained they'd left to go and get a kebab around the same time he'd come to talk to me. I felt a small thrill that he'd picked me over a box of questionable meat.

Our usual table lay empty when we got to Craig's the next night, and right next to it sat Liam and three good-looking guys. One had an extreme case of sunburn, but the other two were the type who coated themselves in oil to achieve the deepest tan possible. Their skin resembled the mahogany bar stools.

It worked out perfectly – four of us and four of them. The girls took the time to speak to each of them before pairing off. I didn't foresee sparks flying, but it felt nice to be in a large group and not have the pressure of entertaining my friends and filling the silences.

With it being our last night, Liam asked for my number so that we could meet up when he got back. I still felt apprehensive – he lived around an hour away by train, and when it came to long-distance romance, I would always be on the pessimistic side.

Again – you're almost halfway through this book by now, so you know my reasons.

One Sex on the Beach later, I conceded and scrawled it on a bar receipt, and the night flew by all too quickly. All I gave him was a quick peck before we headed back to our apartment to pack. He promised to text me the minute he landed at Edinburgh Airport. I took that promise with a grain of salt – after all, another week remained of half-naked lassies parading about. It wouldn't be hard to forget me with the amount of arse crack on display.

True to his word though, a week later at 8.13 p.m., as I lounged on the couch watching a rerun of *One Tree Hill*, a strange number popped up on my screen.

I'm back. How's it going? Love, Scottish guy x

Cute… and unexpected, since I hadn't been holding my breath for the last seven days hoping to hear from him.

OK, that's a small lie – I'd checked the arrivals schedule at Edinburgh Airport that morning. I knew his flight had ended up being delayed by an hour, which meant, if he stayed true to his word, instead of texting between 6 and 7 p.m., I could expect one between 8 and 9 p.m. He would never know that I'd spent needless time working that out. It bordered on pathetic.

I waited ten minutes before writing back, in an attempt to not seem desperate. *It's going well, hope you didn't miss me too much. Love, the lassie who cries* ☺

Everyone berated me for it, but I never put kisses at the end of texts, emails or any form of digital communication. I'd never been a kissy person. If you did put kisses as standard and then happened to forget one, just once, people tended to read into it and think you'd fallen out with them. So I didn't do it. Ever. Whoever I ended up marrying would have to live with it.

Our back and forth went on for two days before he offered to come through and meet me in Glasgow that weekend. He asked if I fancied the cinema. I didn't – not for a first official date – but Liam had offered to travel through to make my life easier, so I compromised.

When I walked out of the train station, he was sitting on a pillar, staring at his phone. It jarred seeing him in 'normal' clothes – I'd half expected the shorts and flip-flops he'd been wearing when we'd first met. I wondered how many girls he'd spoken to after I'd left. How many – much smaller than mine – arse cracks had been wiggled in his face during 'Loch Lomond'?

Don't think about it, I scolded myself. *He's endured a Friday-night train journey and the ramblings of junkies because he likes you.*

His face, when he spotted me, confirmed it. Despite the miserable weather, his huge teeth sparkled in a smile. We had a half hour to kill before the film started and chose to take refuge in a bar next to the station.

I found out he worked as a prison guard, and he talked about his training in great detail. I kept waiting for him to ask me questions about my life. Turns out he wasn't interested enough to ask.

After his third story of how he'd restrained an out-of-control prisoner, I thanked the Lord we were going to the cinema. It would mean I didn't have to listen to his version of *The Shawshank Redemption*.

He continued to drone on about headlocks up until the moment it came to leave. The bill arrived and I offered to pay it since Liam wasn't forthcoming. He'd already informed me the cinema tickets he'd pre-booked cost £20. I took the not-so-subtle hint that I owed him £10 and handed the cash over in exchange for the ticket.

Liam came to an abrupt halt when we stepped into the damp air. 'You want to see how I did it?'

He hadn't held the door open for me so I couldn't be sure I'd heard him right. 'What?'

Liam shivered with excitement. 'How I put someone in a headlock? Then see if you can get out of it?'

It didn't take me long to think about that one. 'Nope.'

'C'mon,' he pushed. 'Bet you can't.' And with no other warning, his Highland cow arms were around my neck, and my body folded in half. The contents of my handbag poured onto the wet pavement.

'Aw, you're not even trying,' he teased, wiggling his arm a little. 'I'm not even doing it that hard.'

I struggled and tried to claw at his arm, which had the circumference of a bull's neck. I knew he wouldn't try to hurt me, but panic started to swell. I didn't enjoy being restrained in any context.

A voice bellowed from down the street, 'Hoi, what the fuck are you playing at?'

Another voice – this time closer: 'Leave the lassie alone.'

Yes, please leave this lassie alone. I just wanted to go on a boring date to the pictures and then change my phone number.

'It's cool,' Liam shouted back, 'just a joke.'

A joke? Then why did I feel like a sheep about to be sheared?

'Nnn…' I huffed.

'Joke's over, pal,' an authoritative voice piped up from somewhere to my right.

Liam's arm released me immediately. When I straightened up, I came face to face with two cops. They didn't look happy.

Liam looked mortified. 'Look, it's nothing, just showing her something from my work.'

Without speaking, the bigger of the two cops grabbed Liam's arms and cuffed them behind his back.

'You can show the guys down at the station then,' the other cop said with a poker-straight face.

Then Liam did the worst thing he could've done under the circumstances – he started to mouth off at both of them. Then he started to struggle when they attempted to lead him away. By this time, bystanders were emerging from the surrounding pubs to enjoy the show. It wasn't a Friday night in Glasgow unless someone ended up being huckled.

Before I could speak up, Liam kicked one of the officers in the legs. With one move, the cop holding him put him face down on the ground, while the other radioed it in. My dad was a cop so I knew he was in for a rough night.

The crowd swelled, and some of them – filled with bravery and Jack Daniel's – were shouting out insults or urging them to 'let the poor bastard go'.

I didn't know what to do – it was becoming a mob scene, and the cops were struggling to control it. Someone launched a bottle from the back of the crowd, which landed just shy of Liam's head, hovering above a puddle. I hoped it was a rain puddle and not the urine kind. The cops had forgotten all about me, and Liam still wouldn't calm down, attempting to kick out at anyone who came near him.

My two options: one – stay, and potentially get glassed in the head and/or hauled to the police station; two – leave and go to the pictures as planned.

The ticket Liam had handed over was burning a hole in my pocket so I went with two, secure in the knowledge that without my statement, they'd let him go, after roughing him up a bit for resisting arrest.

I felt a small pang of guilt as I munched on my hot dog. But then I thought, *What kind of dick puts a girl in a headlock?*

I never went on a girls' holiday again.

Pop Goes the Spot

Stuart and I made it to five dates – a record for me that year. I'd just turned seventeen which meant I needed a 'mature' man. Stuart turned out to be four months and thirteen days older, but beggars can't be choosers.

Five dates meant coming to my house to meet Mum and Dad. If he managed to pass that test, I was considering letting him cop a feel over my FILA hoodie (in 2002 this was considered fashionable; today it would be the equivalent of a crop top with a hint of underboob, farmer wellies and XXXL joggers – or anything an ex-*Love Island*er would wear).

Stuart lasted well under a forty-five-minute interrogation/'now we're just curious' from my parents – who were fooling nobody. Finally, Dad gave me the nod that we were allowed to go upstairs with a firm reminder to 'keep the door open'.

As if I would even waste my time closing it. My mother in random intervals (aided by an egg timer) would rush up the stairs and enter my room claiming to be on the hunt for tweezers, her swimming costume (in January – and she hadn't been in a pool since I'd turned six) or my personal favourite – a pencil. To put that in context, my dad's office was next door and his desk was littered with a variety of writing instruments. Failing that, there was a magnetic notepad stuck to the fridge with a pencil attached. She didn't fool me.

Given I'm a parent now, I wouldn't even be as coy – I'm much more at risk of barging into my daughter's bedroom and kicking said youth square in the balls. Correction – in between the legs since I've no idea of her future sexual preference.

So my door remained wide open. I couldn't bring myself to get too comfortable because I couldn't predict when Mum would shuffle by and gawk in. So instead, I sat cross-legged against the headboard while Stuart kept a respectable distance at the other end of the bed, his trainers planked on the carpet in case he had to dash off.

During the first forty minutes of *Scary Movie 2* – we didn't have Netflix then so we would buy pirated DVDs from the market at four for a tenner – we stayed put. Every once in a while, Stuart would lean back and pat my leg or wink. Ah the teenage hormones were surging through me, and I'd deemed myself ready to be felt up. But his hands – far bigger than they should have been at seventeen years old – stayed in his pockets.

I recalled him mentioning his dad, who worked as a brickie, had hands like shovels, then smirked behind my hand, thinking, *I've got something I wouldn't mind him shovelling.*

I decided to take action, so I shuffled myself to the edge of the bed and gave him a coy smile. His eyes were fixated on the screen where Tori Spelling was getting banged by a ghost. No really, I'm serious. If you don't believe me, go watch it. Before it gets cancelled by millennials because it's offensive to ghosts.

I coughed – hard.

Stuart still didn't look. I couldn't have picked a worse moment. Tori was being banged up against a wall. Riveting.

I coughed again. Stuart shifted his weight and removed the hand closest to me from his pocket. My breath caught. He was going to make a move.

I arched my back so that my modest 34Bs made the F and A in FILA jut out. Stuart gave me a quick grin then went back to watching Tori, his left hand lifting to his face instead of my chest. His index finger scratched at a spot on his left cheek. The scratching turned the whole area scarlet. Then he started clawing at it with two fingers. I averted my gaze to the TV until I thought it may be safe to turn back.

Without speaking, he got up and walked over to the mirror that hung behind my door. I could see in the reflection that his eyes were examining the offending spot, but the door cast a shadow. One of his size thirteens kicked it shut. Now the ceiling light could shine on his face like a stage spotlight.

'What are you doing?' I tried to sound as if I had no clue that he was choosing to pick at his face instead of getting off with his girlfriend. He should've considered himself lucky I didn't get insecure like other girls in our class.

Stuart didn't turn around. 'Be there in a minute.'

Pick, pick, pick – he'd found another one on the hairline at his forehead.

'You might miss Tori Spelling giving a blowjob,' I retorted, hoping he'd pick up on my sarcasm and show me the same attention his fingers were showing his left cheek.

He didn't miss a beat. 'We can rewind it.' His tone told me he wasn't kidding.

I watched as he gave up on the scratching and placed a finger on each side of the spot, mouth open and tongue out as he squeezed.

Nothing happened.

He frowned and squeezed harder.

POP. A huge blob of yellow pus exploded all over my mirror.

Stuart breathed a sigh of relief.

A loud *humph* escaped my mouth before I could stop it.

That startled him. He followed my gaze to the snail-like trail of pus running down the glass. The thick consistency meant if it landed on the carpet, it would be hellish to get out.

'Don't worry, doll – I'll clean it,' he assured me, and with no hesitation, he scooped it up with his finger and proceeded to lick it off. Looking proud as he did so.

This must be what a stroke feels like, I thought. I had a boy in my room who was choosing to suck up his bodily fluid like a snack instead of trying to take advantage of me.

With no warning, the bedroom door flew open, and Mum pounced in, hoping to catch me in flagrante. Instead, she found Stuart sucking his fingers and my face filled with repulsion, mouth still hanging open – like Tori Spelling when she's giving that ghost a blowjob.

Mum surveyed the room, hands planked square on her hips. 'Why is the door shut? Did we not warn you?'

I nodded. 'Stuart did it.' It struck me that I didn't feel the slightest pang of guilt at throwing him under the bus. I just wanted him and his manky fingers out of my room so I could wipe the mirror down and brush my teeth. Did he do that every time he popped a spot? Eat it?

Bile rose in my throat when I remembered all the times I'd kissed him. What if he'd given me tongue herpes? Ugh.

Stuart's neck flushed. 'I'm so sorry – I knocked it shut when I was looking in the mirror.'

Dad must have sensed the possibility of high jinks; he appeared behind Mum. 'What happened?'

Mum gestured to Stuart. 'I came up and found the door shut. Stuart said he did it so he could get a better look in the mirror.'

Stuart pointed to the crater on his cheek. 'Burst a spot – it was annoying me.'

Mum folded her arms and sighed. 'You shut the door… to burst a spot?' She and I both knew what was about to happen.

Dad's eyebrows knitted together. 'Son, I've heard a lot of excuses in my time, but that is the biggest load of shit ever. I used to be a teenage boy; I know what you were up to.'

Stuart held his hands up. 'Mr Paton, I can assure you… it's not—'

Dad fixed his eyes on me. 'And don't think I've forgotten about you.'

I gulped. 'OK.' Fuck.

'I don't appreciate being disrespected in my own house. We have rules for a reason. I think you better get home, Stuart, and I don't want you seeing my daughter anymore.'

Stuart looked to me for help, and I feigned a sad expression, though inside I was dancing with glee. Dad didn't know it, but he'd just given me a 'get out of this relationship' card.

'You better go,' I muttered, trying to sound upset.

Mum gave me one of her sceptical looks as I tried to force out a tear. Nothing came so I resorted to sniffing and looking at the floor.

I heard the rustling of Stuart's jacket as he lifted it off my desk chair and then the heavy tread of his size thirteens as he walked downstairs and through the hall, fading until the front door slammed shut.

Mum and Dad moved to sit on either side of me. 'Sorry we had to do that, but it's for the best. You know the rules,' Mum explained.

'I know what boys are like – that's why we want the door kept open, so we know you're OK. You'll find someone else,' Dad said, patting me on the shoulder.

Little did he know I'd been the one planning to take advantage of Stuart. But it looked like my 34Bs were destined to go unfondled a little while longer.

Mum still looked unconvinced – after all, she'd seen me kick off for a lot less than my boyfriend being chucked out of the house. 'Are you alright?'

I sniffed louder and nodded. 'I'll be fine. Just need some time alone.'

They took their cue and stood up.

'Bloody bursting a spot – he must think we're idiots.' I could hear Dad chuckling as the two of them walked downstairs. 'Heard it all now.'

I waited until I heard the living-room door click shut and then reached for the desk drawer containing wipes and the bottle of antibacterial spray. Yes, I kept those in my room. Don't judge me for being a clean and germophobic teenager, alright? Most parents would consider me a prize.

I scrubbed that mirror for a good twenty minutes, but I still felt dirty every time I looked into it.

Dad waited till dinner to inform me that I'd been grounded for a week. I figured I owed him that since he'd done me a favour. As for the mirror – it lasted a week before I smashed it with a stapler and told Mum it fell off the wall.

I never did get tongue herpes.

No Stalking on the Grass

Graeme was introduced to me through a friend of a friend. At this stage, I should have been looking for new friends because they were fucking useless at matchmaking.

This tale is a short and sweet one, because it may have taken me a few years to get there, but at twenty-three I now possessed the ability to spot a lunatic. Therefore, I knew when to push the metaphorical eject button and parachute to safety. In this case, it involved ejecting myself from the passenger seat of his car.

Not knowing me at all, Graeme had taken me to a pretentious four-star restaurant called Grapevine. The place stank of jasmine, and after ten minutes I'd seen more male ankles than I'd ever thought possible. The craze of men wearing stiff loafers and no socks had just begun. It continues to this day.

To be fair to him he did ask me a load of questions, seemed interested in my answers and didn't come across as only wanting one thing. However, I felt nothing. Like when the guy would come to read the electric meter – I'd just let him in the front door, watch him take a reading and then show him right back out. Nothing. Couldn't even tell you the colour of his hair. Just a blur in a high-vis vest.

I made as much effort as I could, disappointed that I couldn't muster up any feeling whatsoever. I tried to pick something on his face to admire – perhaps talk myself into finding him more than just OK looking. That one thing that makes you want to rip someone's clothes off.

His eyebrows caught my attention – perfect arches of black. Almost too perfect. I considered asking if they'd been waxed. Instead, I nipped my wrist. A distraction technique to stop myself from asking an uncomfortable question or giving an inappropriate answer. For two hours, I managed to engage in pleasant yet dull conversation, listening as he described his sister-in-law's weird obsession with cows – he claimed her entire decorating scheme consisted of black-and-white spatter, including her carpet. She also boasted an impressive china cat collection that his brother wasn't allowed to touch or move from a display cabinet in their bedroom.

My wrist became red raw. My curiosity always got the better of me, and I found myself debating whether I could handle a second date, just in the hope that I could one day visit the weird cow shrine. Anyone who decorated their house that way must be proud enough to show it off, right? But then he changed the subject to how he'd helped his mum change electricity supplier and save £30 a year, and I wished someone would hurl one of those disgusting male loafers at my head and put me out of my misery.

Graeme's one saving grace was that he had a *very* nice Audi. My knowledge of cars ended at them having four wheels and an engine, but even I recognised the four rings on the front from an advert. This one gleamed a shiny red with sparkling alloys, and he'd kept the interior immaculate. It reeked of that new-car showroom smell, which made me think it could indeed be brand new, especially as no tree air freshener dangled from the rear-view.

He went up in my estimation when he rushed around to open the passenger door for me and didn't close it until my seat belt was fastened. Then he sprinted back around to the driver's side as if I'd disappear if he didn't jump in the car quick enough.

We reached my parents' house just over an hour later since he'd chosen a restaurant smack bang in the middle of Edinburgh despite us both living in Wishaw. Cue further talks of energy prices increasing and how he hoped to buy his own flat that year. Graeme embodied it all – polite, attentive, nice car, aspirations in life, and despite his family sounding like they were off their rocker, I could tell he loved them.

Why didn't I find discussions about mortgage base rates and cow ornaments interesting? If I did, I could just marry this guy right now and save myself the torture of even one more dating escapade.

But it wasn't to be. He leaned in to kiss me, and I didn't have enough time to back off, so instead I just let it happen. I thought I owed the guy that much.

I did not owe him the slug trying to mate with my tongue though. You know those shimmery, slimy trails that slugs leave on the pavement that you try to avoid stepping on? Well, imagine the pavement is your face. I feared my chin would be sucked through to the Bermuda Triangle.

It seemed relentless.

Those three seconds of shock lasted what felt like ten life-times before I shoved his shoulders so hard that he flew back against the driver's door.

Damn – those triceps curls I'd been doing in my room for the last week had paid off!

'I have to go,' I screeched, grappling to unclip my seat belt.

Graeme made a quick recovery. 'Are you sure?' He pulled the zip down on his jacket and stretched an arm behind the passenger seat.

I gulped. 'Never been as sure in my life. Thanks for dinner.'

Seat belt now unclipped, I bolted for the safety of my front door. Manners forced me to turn and wave as I waited for him to drive off.

He didn't – and made no move to fasten his seat belt either. Instead, he just peered through the passenger window, watching me. With one last wave, I stumbled into the house and locked the door behind me, including the extra snib.

After using two baby wipes on my face to remove the remaining drool, I headed for the shower and spent a good fifteen minutes and a whole jar of pricey facial scrub to make me feel clean again. Ugh, I could almost taste the ravioli and garlic bread he'd ordered in the restaurant.

Showered, dried and dressed in new pyjamas that I'd been saving since Christmas, I decided to make some toast before bed. Yes, I save pyjamas because I like the 'new' feeling right before you wash them – before they start to fall apart and lose their cosiness. It's an affliction.

As I waited for the toast to pop, I wandered into the living room to make sure nothing had been left on. Mum had messaged me earlier to say she'd gone to bed early with a migraine, and Dad had been called in for a nightshift. I still liked to check everything as a force of habit, in case they'd missed a light or a lock on a window.

Dawdling engine noise from the driveway caught my attention. I knew it couldn't be Dad as he parked out on the street, so Mum didn't have to move his car in the morning.

The driveway light glinted off four shiny rings. Graeme had pulled the car into our drive, and I watched him eyeing up each window. I went into the kitchen and grabbed my phone off the counter. The clock above our cooker showed 11 p.m. – almost forty-five minutes after he'd dropped me off.

Why are you still outside? I texted.

I wanted to wait and see if you changed your mind.

Graeme needed to learn to take a hint.

I told you no thanks. I'm going to bed. You should go home.

My phone pinged within seconds. *I'll give it another half hour.*

Give what another half hour? Time for the police to turn up? Oh wait, my dad was the police, so if I phoned them about this creep, there was a good chance he would be the one barrelling down our street in a patrol car.

It became clear that Graeme also didn't understand normal social parameters. In the real world, when someone dives out of your car, running for their life, you don't hang around to see if they want a repeat of the episode that prompted it. Now I'd have to be a bitch to get my point across.

Don't waste your time. Leave. And delete my number.

The toast popped up, and I buttered it, keeping one eye on my phone screen. Ten minutes later, I heard the Audi rev and saw the headlights flick across the living-room wall as he reversed out of the driveway. There was still no reply.

I deliberated on my harsh response as I walked upstairs, chewing. I finished both slices before pulling back my covers and rearranging my pillows just how I liked them. Crumbs in your bed should be used instead of waterboarding as a form of torture.

Graeme followed my instructions. He left, perhaps deleting my number before he turned the ignition.

Yet I couldn't help myself.

I found myself picking up my phone, hesitating before typing, *Could you send me your sister-in-law's number? I'd love to see her house.*

That elicited a response: *Fuck off.*

Now I'd never get to see that cow-spatter decorating scheme.

Napkin Guy

The most glorious year to be a teenager was no doubt 2001. Not for the dating scene, mind you. But because it birthed the era of Britney Spears, Skechers and getting your make-up from the front of magazines featuring blonde-tipped boybands. The blue hair mascara streaked through my locks came from one of said magazines. Back then they cost like £2.

So, at sixteen, I'd been on the dating scene for a year. Officially. According to my dad. Unofficially – and to everyone else, including my mother – I'd been dating for three years. Nothing serious, just a couple of kisses followed by a quick chest grope that I would shut down in a heartbeat.

Opportunities to meet boys were abundant at this age – school, my cousins' school, my cousins' street, the shopping centre, oh and random walks around the area. With no social media to hide behind, all interactions were face to face, unless you added people onto your MSN messenger. If you were born after 1995, ask your parents what that is. Your username could convey everything from your mood to the lassie you hated at school.

A week before the schools went back in August, my parents decided to throw a barbeque. When I say parents, I mean my mother, because three days prior to it, a new wicker patio set arrived. From a catalogue. Yes, people also ordered things from catalogues in 2001. You didn't get to look at a screen and check it out from different angles. You just trusted that the one picture stuck in the corner of the page would be what the product looked like on arrival. Even with clothes, though I could never quite pull off a knitted jumpsuit the same way the *Kays Catalogue* model did.

Barbeque day that Saturday dawned bright and clear – there'd been an unprecedented heatwave that had lasted the whole week, though the forecast predicted it would end the day school started. Mum allowed me to invite four friends – since she'd invited half of the street, her bingo chums, choir friends and Dad's police buddies.

We'd lived on our street since I was five, but I only knew the name of one lot of neighbours – my best friend and her family, who lived four doors down. Everyone else remained a faceless blur that I'd see on my walk to the school bus every morning, or if I happened to peep out my bedroom window as they carried messages into their house.

Dad manned the barbecue while Mum ran back and forth with bowls of burger buns and potato salad, gesturing for me to hand out the pile of utensils she'd prewrapped in napkins. I'd told her to just stick the plastic cutlery in a big bowl, but that idea had been shot down in flames. My mother considered herself a host to rival Martha Stewart, so everything had to be perfect – even the plastic cutlery that a mere ten percent of the guests would use. Also, in 2001, we didn't have any regard for the planet whatsoever. Even our hair looked plastic, thanks to the abundance of Silvikrin hairspray being blasted up at the ozone layer.

Halfway through the afternoon, a six-foot blonde with her hair in a chignon arrived, pulling behind her a reluctant brown-haired teen around my age. His hair resembled that of Nick Carter from the Backstreet Boys – who'd featured on the front of the magazine I'd purchased with the hair mascara.

Coincidence? Perhaps. But in my sixteen-year-old brain, it was a sign I was destined to marry this guy. My imagination took over: a daydream of snow-white Skechers on my feet peeping out from underneath an A-line dress of lace and tulle. I'd float down the aisle towards his sallow skin and dimples, smiling acknowledgement to the guests as I passed.

Mum snapped me out of my daydream right at the moment he took me in his arms for our first dance as a married couple. Song of choice? Westlife's 'Flying Without Wings'.

Her arms flailed from the other end of the garden. 'Nicola, get over here.'

The sound of my friends' giggling followed as I tried to stride across the grass in my combat trousers and gingham crop top with confidence – not to be confused with the crop tops you see now, because in 2001, the ones we wore covered our breasts. They didn't poke out from the bottom or the sides. They remained under wraps.

Mum's foot tapped as I approached, a sign that I had taken too long. 'This is Megan – she just joined the choir. Turns out she lives around the corner,' Mum announced like this was the news I'd been waiting for all my life.

Megan looked about as happy to meet me as I was her. 'Nice to meet you,' I muttered.

'You too,' Megan responded, checking her hot-pink nails as she did so. 'This is Ford, my son.' She shoved him forward, more interested in the chipped nail she'd discovered than her offspring.

Mum's eyes danced between us. 'You're about the same age – why don't you go and get him a drink?' Mum gestured to the back door leading into the kitchen.

Ford had yet to talk. Or even acknowledge my existence. Couldn't he tell that his future wife was standing in front of him? He should have been taking all this in so he could recount it to our grandkids in the nursing home. Because he'd been too heartbroken to live in our house after I'd died. He'd also tell them how he'd stroked my hair as I took my last breath, at peace in our bed while the sun went down…

'Nicola,' Mum barked.

I jumped. 'What? Oh yeah, do you want a drink?' I directed the question at my soulmate through a dry mouth. I hoped he'd say yes so I could down a pint of water myself and pull it together.

Ford shrugged. 'Why not?' And then loped behind me as I made my way to the back door and into our kitchen.

I yanked the fridge open and shoved my head inside to give the illusion I was scanning it for the perfect beverage. In reality, I needed it to cool down my flushed cheeks and give myself a stern talking-to.

He's just a boy, I grumbled in my head, banging some cans around while Ford eyed up the pictures on our kitchen noticeboard. *Nothing to be scared of. You are pretty.* I straightened my shoulders. *Maybe not as pretty as Stacy Murphy* – my current MSN messenger username stated 'Stacy Murphy is a stuck-up bitch' – *but you are acceptable. Ford would be lucky to date you.*

'Did you say something?' Ford peered around the door and wore a concerned/who-is-this-weirdo expression.

I picked up the first bottle I put my hands on. 'Yup, just looking for this. It's my favourite – do you like it?'

His brow furrowed. 'Your favourite drink is goat's milk?'

I followed his gaze to the bottle I held up, and sure enough, it turned out to be a bottle of goat's milk.

Shit. We didn't even drink goat's milk – how did such a thing find its way into our fridge?

Auntie Julie walked by the kitchen window three seconds later. Auntie Julie was dairy intolerant and drank a cup of tea every fifteen minutes, no matter how high the temperature. Like today.

Fucking Auntie Julie. She'd just found herself the target of my next MSN username.

This situation required some major blagging. 'Uh yeah, it's so refreshing. And healthy, mmmm.' I feigned delight as best I could then shoved it back into the fridge shelf from whence it came.

Ford wore the look of someone who feared I may waterboard him with my disgusting beverage. 'I'll just take a Pepsi if you have it.'

Back went my face into the fridge, where I found one whole shelf had been dedicated to Pepsi. Why couldn't my hand have landed on that?

With a popular and safe beverage in his hands, Ford leaned back against the kitchen island and snapped the ring off. I banged the fridge door shut and jumped up onto the counter.

'You not having a drink?' he asked, taking huge swigs without stopping. Even his Adam's apple called to me.

'Uh, sure, yup,' I babbled, jumping back down so I could pull a matching can out of the fridge.

His eyes darted from the can to my face. 'I thought you said the goat's milk was your favourite – you not having that?'

Auntie Julie was getting a dead rat in the mouth of a pigeon for Christmas. She'd destroyed the most important non-date of my so-far-short life.

'Yes, it is. I thought you'd maybe want another since you're drinking that so quick.' I made a big show of walking over and placing it on the counter next to the now-empty Pepsi with a big smile.

Then I lifted a glass out of the cupboard, retrieved the milk and tentatively poured out half a glass. It smelled like the underside of a goat. I'd never even known you *could* milk a goat; I dreaded to think what their nipples looked like.

It took a lot of willpower not to retch at the cloudiness in the glass; I needed fresh air.

'You want to head back outside?' As much as I wanted to keep him in here all to myself, my nose told me that wasn't going to work for my stomach.

He gave a non-committal shrug as I walked past him and headed to a picnic table Mum had set up for me and my friends. It happened to be located at the far end of the garden and therefore out of earshot of her friends, in case I happened to say something embarrassing – like I would reveal at a barbecue that she liked to use my dad's razor for shaving her neck or something.

My four friends stood in line for the hamburgers and hot dogs Dad dished up at a much slower pace than people were used to. I watched my mum's choir pal start hopping from foot to foot, either desperate for a chicken wing or the toilet.

Ford slid his legs under the table in one fluid motion. A sharp contrast to me – I looked like someone trying to fold a giraffe into an egg box. Being able to fit into a cheap plastic folding table was a skill I'd not yet acquired.

Now what?

My eyes caught the food-laden table to the right of us. 'Do you like potato salad?'

Blank brown eyes.

I took this lack of response as a cue to continue. 'Ugh, I can't stand it. Even if I did like it, I couldn't have it – would set my IBS off big time. Same with brown bread. Love the stuff but can't touch it.'

His blank brown eyes grew wider, yet he didn't turn away. In my excited and almost hysterical state, it didn't dawn on me that those eyes were drifting over to stare at the tree behind me as I prattled on for ten minutes about how IBS left me chained to the toilet for hours.

Looking back, I'm sure he envisaged himself hanging from that tree as a way to escape the hellish monologue that my mouth couldn't stop spewing.

My listing of stomach issues stopped when my friends appeared next to the table, laden down with paper plates filled with meat and the offending potato salad.

'This is Ford,' I informed them, annoyed that they hadn't taken my not-so-subtle nods to sit at another table so that I could hold his full attention. All four of my friends were – in my opinion – a lot prettier than me, and therefore a threat to mine and Ford's blossoming relationship.

All four gave him coy smiles with straight white teeth – in contrast to my crooked mouth, which showed just a bit too much gum for my liking.

A brainwave. 'We were just going to grab some food so why don't you guys take this table? It'll be too crowded for six of us anyway.'

I may have needed five minutes to climb into the thing, but it took me only thirty seconds to get out and run round to pull Ford up.

His eyes widened to reach his thick eyebrows – two shades lighter than his hair. 'H-Honest, I'm not that hungry,' he stammered, resisting my hand on his arm.

I tightened my grip, not willing to let the opportunity to get him alone again pass me by. 'Once you try my dad's hot dogs, you'll change your mind. C'mon.' And with a vicious yank, I freed him from the table and marched him over to the back of the line.

Mum sped up the doling-out process by telling Dad that he'd better, well, in not so many words, hurry up. This meant we waited in the queue for less than a minute. I took the opportunity to show off what a good girlfriend I would be by gathering a plate, napkin and cutlery for him. I even went so far as to scoop a big heap of potato salad onto the plate, which in hindsight I should have checked if he liked. After my IBS speech, he'd neither confirmed nor denied his feelings on the subject of potato salad.

I kept up a running commentary of how long we'd lived here, how long the garden renovations had lasted, and despite my mother's threats to not reveal we'd bought the patio set from a catalogue, I confessed in hushed tones that my parents were in fact 'paying it up'.

I took his silence as a confirmation that he would never reveal we'd bought furniture on 'credit' – another taboo word I'd been forbidden from uttering today.

Dad stood over the grill, turning the kebab skewers. 'What are you having?' he directed to Ford, beaming with pride at the feast he'd been placed 'in charge of'. If he'd known what my plans were for Ford, I doubt he'd have been smiling. Ford's head would've been the thing turning on a skewer with peppers either side.

Ford took his time looking over everything on offer. 'I'll have a burger, two chicken wings, one of those kebabs and a corn on the cob,' he confirmed with a nod.

Dad looked impressed. 'Somebody's hungry.'

As Dad started to slide the requested items onto Ford's plate, I noticed the oversight. 'Oh, you forgot to get a hot dog. Dad, give him a hot dog,' I trilled.

Ford grimaced. 'I don't like hot dogs.'

Dad replaced the tongs he'd lifted. 'It's fine, son. Not to everyone's taste.'

My pig-headed adolescent brain couldn't let it go. 'You'll like these. Dad uses a special seasoning on them – you won't regret it.'

I leaned over the table, lifted the tongs and selected the longest hot dog on the grill before grabbing a bun, slipping the sausage inside and dousing the whole thing in ketchup and mustard. Again, I didn't stop to ask if Ford even wanted any condiments on his food.

My future husband stared at the offending mess I'd slapped on his plate. His broad shoulders slumped as Dad placed a single plain hamburger on my empty plate. He knew me well – I hated all condiments except salt.

'Let's eat over here.' I pulled Ford by the elbow towards our conservatory stairs, which placed us in the shade and away from watchful eyes.

He battled against me, his face turned to the crowd, perhaps hoping for his mother to come rescue him. But she was busy regaling a group of Dad's friends with some story involving a motorbike and a rabbit which caused the crowd to erupt in laughter every few seconds.

He didn't proclaim with rapturous delight that it was indeed the best hot dog he'd ever tasted – instead, he shuffled everything else on his plate to one side so that it rolled itself over to the edge. To fill the uneasy silence, I tried to coax him into playing a guessing game of what Dad's special ingredient could be. I prattled off every spice I could remember seeing in my mum's spice rack. 'Maybe it's oregano?' I raised my voice at the end so that he'd sense the question and therefore answer. Or at least speak.

Despite the shade, the heat still made droplets of sweat form above my lip, causing my brown lip liner (from last month's magazine) to run and no doubt ruin my make-up. This, combined with the silent treatment, irritated me. 'You're not very talkative, are you?'

My bluntness didn't faze him – instead, he whipped out a pen from an invisible pocket on his combats, unfurled the napkin in his left hand and scrawled something. With a pointed dab, he finished and held it in the air for me to read.

I would talk but I can't get a word in.

Sweat felt like it now dripped out of every pore. 'How dare you. Maybe I wouldn't have to do all the talking if you had something interesting to say. Or anything at all. You're so boring. Ugh, I can't believe I liked you.'

Reading this now, I bet you're thinking, *That's the best insult she could come up with? Boring?* But again, it was 2001 – I hadn't been exposed to a lot of colourful language yet, and the words I did know, I couldn't repeat surrounded by a group of cops and rock-choir members.

He didn't even respond to that – his mouth just stayed clamped shut in a smirk. I lifted one of the chicken wings off his plate and threw it at his feet before flouncing off. Immature and unnecessary, as I would just have to go back and clean it up after everyone left.

I rarely saw him around the neighbourhood after that – perhaps because he was doing his best to avoid me or because my mum now couldn't socialise with his. She'd been barred after I lied to Dad and told him Ford had badmouthed his hot dog, saying it tasted like dog shit covered in ketchup.

So for those of you thinking that liking boys must have been easier in the days before social media – think again.

The Big Ex

Dean and I met on his first shift working at McDonald's. I'd been there a couple of months by that point; it was the first real job I'd applied for the minute my National Insurance card landed on the doormat, and I considered myself a professional already. The fast pace of, well, fast food meant you could either hack it or you couldn't, and of the twelve people at my induction, only I remained. Despite crying for an hour before and after my first four shifts, I couldn't bring myself to quit. Not when I made enough money to warrant opening a bank account along with the guarantee of four free large meals a week – including a McFlurry.

Dean is not to be confused with Steven, who you've read about in a previous story. Remember the bathmat guy? I mean, how could you forget?

Steven started working at McDonald's during my second year. At that stage, I'd become part of the furniture and an expert at grabbing and eating a chicken nugget every time I walked by the nugget drawer. Dean arrived at a time when I still couldn't figure out which fryer kept beeping.

So, Dean found himself on a shift with me at the counter, where I'd been tasked with training him on the drinks dispenser. A task that turned out to bond us due to our sheer hatred of the damn machine. Its unpredictability meant it either doused your hand in Coke or sputtered for three minutes only to produce two drops of Sprite while the customer tutted behind us.

However, he made me laugh during the monotony, even when one irate customer threw her cup of Diet Coke at me, claiming that she'd ordered full-fat Coke – though a scan of the receipt once I'd cleaned myself up proved that she had, indeed, ordered a Diet Coke. Dean felt sorry for me and tried to take the blame when our floor manager pulled me aside and asked what the hell had gone wrong. This particular manager always caught me nicking a chicken nugget as I headed back to the storeroom, so I was already on thin ice. I thought I'd perfected the art of being stealthy but obviously not.

Dean threw himself into the fryer for me – see what I did there? – and took responsibility, stating he must've mixed up the order with another set of drinks for a previous customer. It sounded believable since he still wore a trainee badge, though it made me seem like a shit teacher – but I could live with that.

His intentions seemed honourable – risking his job during an induction period for a girl whom he'd shown no interest in except to comment once that the disgusting checked shirt they made us wear wasn't 'all that bad' on me.

I found myself checking the floor plan at the start of each shift; sometimes if the schedule went up the night before, I would scan it before leaving. Depending on whether his name appeared, I'd either skip home or trudge up the hill. On the occasions Mum and Dad picked me up, they could tell my mood by whether I slammed the car door or dived into the passenger seat beaming. They didn't know that it was all to do with a boy – Mum attributed my good moods to the McFlurrys, while Dad put them down to me having more money for clothes.

A perk yes, but working with Dean made shifts go a lot faster. When his induction period ended and I knew we wouldn't be working side by side anymore, I felt beaten. The worst part was that I couldn't figure out whether he felt the same. He kept his jokes hilarious, yet platonic. I never felt his hands graze over my arse when he reached past me to grab straws from under the counter. There were no tantalising looks as we hung out at the drive-thru window at the end of a dark corridor. Oh, the things I'd fantasised about during those shifts. They were definitely an affront to the family-friendly ethos of McDonald's – Ronald McDonald would've kicked me out if he'd had any idea what was going on in my mind.

It didn't help that one of the floor managers – Caitlin – seemed to have it out for me and scheduled Dean and me on opposite shifts. Just as I'd be finishing the breakfast shift and cleaning up syrup, Dean would come around the corner, lugging a bag of hamburger patties over his shoulder. It sounds insane lusting after someone for how they carried hamburger meat – but I did.

Twelve shifts later – while Caitlin was on holiday – I'd taken a shift swap for a Thursday night so I could go to my best friend's birthday party on Saturday. I'd stopped checking the schedule for Dean's name, resigning myself to the fact that the McDonald's god had spoken. And by god I mean the corporate office, who frowned upon any hints of fraternisation between the staff – not that anyone paid attention. The few work nights out I'd attended were more an excuse for PG-rated orgies than celebrating Ashley's promotion to shift manager.

Yet when I rounded the corner to clock in, the gods had chosen to smile upon me. Dean stood in front of the keypad, punching in his work number – looking adorable in the dumb black hat they made us wear that left the top part of your hair a mop of sweat when you removed it during your break.

We both smiled, said nothing and went to our respective stations. I'd been trained on tills, and despite numerous requests to have kitchen training, it had never happened. Perhaps my penchant for chicken nuggets meant they worried I would eat more than I cooked. Dean – despite having been trained for the front counter his entire induction period – had been moved to the kitchen, specializing in making cheeseburgers.

His station sat behind the front counter, meaning every time I turned to grab a bag or use the drinks machine, I could peep through and see him. A glimpse of dark hair on well-defined forearms. A strong hand with neat nails that flipped patties with record speed. Twice, I'd been so distracted watching him that I'd flooded the counter with orange juice, failing to notice the cup having filled to the brim.

If Caitlin hadn't been in Tenerife, then the ice I now stood on would be glacier thin. Thankfully, Ross – a junior floor manager – gave the impression of always being stoned, and as long as the place didn't burn down and our tills added up at the end of the night, he didn't give a shit. Somehow, mine would always be five pence down – every time.

During a lull around 8 p.m., Ross tasked me with stocking up, which translated to me doing all the work while he sat in the office and read the paper. Or smoked. Who knew what went on behind that mirrored door given that he could see out, but we couldn't see in?

Grabbing an empty ketchup basket, I made a last check that no one was about to walk in the front door before I headed to the storeroom – a dark, cold, sickly-sweet place piled high with boxes and cartons of syrups and soft-drink canisters. The smell could delight you when found in a hot fudge sundae, but twenty boxes of the stuff in a cramped room with no ventilation would test your gag reflex.

The door, due to it being a fire door, also had a habit of closing itself, no matter how many boxes you placed in front of it. We'd all been told that constituted a fire hazard, but we didn't listen. We all knew Ross was the real fire hazard.

That night, I didn't bother dragging boxes over to keep it open, allowing some fresh air from the open back door to wander in instead. I accepted my fate and got down to the task of refilling the ketchup basket, one tiny box at a time, in nice, neat stacks. Enjoying the skive, to be honest.

I'd made myself a good seat by placing a large pack of straws on top of a box of salt sachets. It didn't occur to me that the straws would be crushed under my weight.

Well, it did, but for £7.50 an hour, I didn't care. So there I sat in my comfy hiding place until Dean found me, hiding behind a tower of boxes I'd constructed.

He'd removed his hat, displaying the matted mess of strawberry-blonde hair underneath. 'Skiving again?' he asked, smirking.

My piles of ketchup were abandoned. 'You going to grass me in?' I joked. My left foot started to tap, and I tucked it behind a box.

He folded his arms and squared his feet. 'Maybe. Can't have you wasting valuable company time. That's not the McDonald's motto.'

I played along, simpering, 'Oh, so what is the motto?'

He paused before stating with conviction, 'Eh, skivemus muchas possible.'

I doubled over with laughter and kicked out my right leg at the same time. Result? An avalanche of napkins was freed from the confines of the box tower.

The sight of a sweat-soaked napkin resting like a paper hat on Dean's hair turned my laughter from a giggle to a roar. He scowled for all of three seconds before joining in.

I straightened myself up, wiping my cheeks before noticing that Dean now stood closer to me. In fact, he'd moved square on in front of me.

'You're pretty when you laugh,' he stated, no longer laughing.

What's the correct response to that? Thanks? Should I sound like I know I'm pretty or be self-deprecating? Would that make it seem like I had no self-confidence?

The minefield of dating – or napkin-field I should say as I surveyed the paper sea of carnage around us and tried to think of something witty to respond with.

The best my brain came up with was: 'That's what they say.'

I'd no idea who 'they' referred to. They did not exist. No one had ever told me that I looked pretty when I laughed, even my dad – and he'd considered me a supermodel at thirteen despite having buck teeth.

I wanted to shoot myself in the face.

Dean didn't appear to care about my daft answer – instead, he took a step closer until I had no option but to turn my face up to his or else conduct a conversation with his chest.

'I'm sure they do,' he teased, his mouth fast approaching mine.

I found myself wishing I'd sucked on a mint after the McChicken Sandwich meal I'd eaten during break. A girl never knew who would creep up on her in a storeroom and accost her while she wore the most hideous and unflattering uniform ever designed.

Too late to do anything now. Or even breathe before he kissed me. It was light at first, then he dared to put his hands on my hips and pull me closer as the kiss deepened. My back arched as I strained not to break contact. At five foot seven, people considered me tall for a girl, but Dean was like an NBA player at six five.

That glorious kiss lasted five minutes before Ross ruined the moment and kicked open the fire door. 'Nicki, I'm going for a fag – get up front.' Yeah, and by fag, he didn't mean the tobacco kind.

The moment broken, we scurried to gather up the mess, choosing to stuff everything into a half-empty box rather than sorting it out. I grabbed my half-filled box of ketchup, Dean shoved his hat back on and in an unspoken agreement, we exited the room ten seconds apart.

I returned to the front counter where – thanks to Ross – a queue of people had converged, explaining his sudden fag break. Which meant Dean and the other two guys in the kitchen were kept busy for the next hour, allowing us no time to discuss what had happened.

It wasn't until the cleaning crew on the night shift appeared that we all managed to down tools and head to the crew room to collect our stuff. Any other time, I couldn't get out of the place fast enough, but I found myself loitering at the back door, urging Dean to hurry up and put his jacket on.

The people who drove ran to their cars, and the people who walked or needed to catch a bus headed in different directions. Dean fell into the walking category, having failed his driving test twice so far. My car – which Dad had bought me for £250 – remained trapped in the garage after I'd complained of the 'brakes sounding funny'. According to the mechanic, the brake pads were thinner than paper, and he couldn't believe I hadn't gone into the back of someone – or something. Checking my watch, I noted Mum would be picking me up in ten minutes, giving me a total of six hundred seconds to find out if that kiss equated to:

- a fluke
- a result of attractive laughter
- a response to the overpowering syrup fumes
- the start of something special

I timed it so that as Dean emerged from the back door, I bent down to fix the lace I'd untied on my black trainers. A cheap ploy, but a reliable one.

He shrugged a Sum 41 backpack over his shoulder and walked towards me, glancing around as he did so. 'You getting picked up?' he asked, looking out the side of his eye.

I followed his line of sight to the chip shop across the street, the logical stop for the people who couldn't be bothered waiting in the drive-thru queue or who'd discovered we were closed. McDonald's didn't always operate 24/7 – we used to close at 11 p.m. and not open again until 7 a.m. Shocking, right? People were forced to find other forms of sustenance during those eight hours. No Deliveroo or Just Eat for my generation – we survived on toast for supper until breakfast the next morning.

A car horn beeped on the main road and brought his eyes back to my face. 'Sorry, thought I saw someone I knew there. Do you want me to walk you home?' The sweet look returned.

Crap! Why had I taken Mum up on her offer of picking me up? Oh right, because I was lazy and hated walking. I couldn't even call her to say I'd make my own way home because hardly anyone owned a mobile phone then. I'll bet technology messed up a lot of these kinds of chances in people's dating lives. Even more than it does now.

I shrugged. 'Sorry, Mum's picking me up.' Playing it back in my head, I realised I hadn't sounded too sorry. 'I mean, I'd love it if you could walk me home, but she'll worry if she turns up and I'm not here.'

A finger lifted my chin, and without warning, he kissed me again. Even though we were in a deserted, dimly lit car park, it left me feeling exposed. I'd always been self-conscious about kissing – or any form of affection – in public. To me, the cars whizzing by on the main street over the fence from us felt like being in a spotlight in Madison Square Garden.

Headlights washed over us as a car turned in and came to a stop, the engine idling. Through the windscreen, I could see Mum smirking and giving me a thumbs up; she may as well have stood up through the sunroof screaming, 'Caught.' She still asked me if I'd got 'a lumber' anytime I went out with my friends. For the longest time, I thought she was asking if I'd met a lumberjack so my response would always be no. Or maybe I have; I'm not sure what one is. My nanny enlightened me with its true meaning after hearing Mum quiz me on my return home one night (an hour after I should've been tucked up in bed and reeking of peach schnapps).

Did you get a lumber? Translation: did you kiss anyone? Otherwise known as a snog, a winch, tonsil hockey.

Dean seemed unfazed by our audience. 'Hope I didn't get you into trouble.' He stepped back and raised his hand in a self-confident I-just-got-caught-kissing-your-teenage-daughter-but-please-don't-run-me-over wave. With the same hand that had been heading south of my waist a few seconds ago.

If I didn't get in the car within seconds, Mum would choose to exit it and either A) introduce herself or B) ask if he was a good kisser.

'You working tomorrow?' I queried, walking backwards to the car.

He'd started doing the furtive glances around again; I put it down to nerves. I'd be a wreck if his mum had pulled up and seen us kissing, with my hand going to a questionable area. It didn't help that mums were usually so protective of their boys – like every girl was a total bitch, no matter what. Yes, Dean's mum would be guaranteed to hate me.

The cars on the main street started to beep at a learner who'd stalled at the lights; I assumed he hadn't heard me. 'Dean? You working tomorrow?'

I almost repeated myself when he responded, 'Ugh, yeah, four-to-eleven shift. You?'

My naïve heart soared. 'Same. See you.'

One last smile and I slid into the car while he walked towards the bus stop.

Mum's smile split her face. 'Oooft, you got a lumber there, eh?'

I sighed. 'Can you just call it kissing like everyone else? It's so bloody annoying. This isn't the sixties.'

She turned the key in the ignition and performed a U-turn to head out of the industrial estate. 'We still let boys grope our arses in the sixties.'

I sank back into the seat and groaned.

Much like the shift the night before, we found ourselves too busy to talk or even exchange eye contact the next day. Also, Caitlin returned from Tenerife – an attractive shade of fuchsia – and placed us on opposite break times. If she hadn't been ten years older and resembled a flamingo, I'd have deduced that she wanted Dean for herself.

Dad dropped me off at the garage that morning to pick my car up, complete with new stiff brakes that caused an emergency stop if my trainer so much as grazed the pedal.

My bright idea to get Dean alone again was to offer him a lift home. I knew that he lived four bus stops away – a mere ten-minute journey if that. As of yet, I'd never kissed anyone in my car – except my gran that time I'd picked her up to go to the garden centre and spent two hours looking at scarves. Please note it was a kiss on the cheek as a thank you for taking her out. Nothing incestuous. This is not that kind of book.

During a lull in the queue, I sneaked behind the fryer to ask him. He accepted my offer with a wink before going back to scraping oil off the grill.

My car didn't afford me any bragging rights, but it was cheap to run and gave me my independence. Which meant I didn't usually have to endure annoying quiz sessions with my mother about anyone she had seen me with.

I felt excited to show Dean my driving – like I'd appear grown-up and cultured since he still took lessons twice a week.

My excitement must have been infectious, as he seemed giddy on our stroll to the back door. Being a gentleman, he motioned for me to go first.

I stopped dead.

Dean slammed into the back of me, and I steadied myself, ignoring the pain from his Timberland boots climbing my ankles.

My tiny blue car, my baby, sat under the same street lamp I always left it under so I could see an attacker coming or find my keys. The shattered windscreen glinted under the light, and the passenger side looked deflated.

My mouth gaped. 'What the hell?' I shrieked, advancing towards the driver's side out of habit for closer inspection. The object that had been used to smash the windscreen remained stuck right in the middle of it.

'Is that a roof tile?' I questioned the night air.

Dean approached on the passenger side. 'Looks like it. Both tyres have been slashed on this side as well.'

I'd never been the victim of vandalism before. 'Who would do this?' I asked Dean, meaning it rhetorically.

His mouth pursed. 'Um, I might have an idea.'

I paused from trying to pull the roof tile out of the windscreen. 'Who? It's not someone we work with – I mean Caitlin can be a bitch, but she'd never do this.'

He took a deep breath as he twisted the McDonald's cap in his hand. 'My ex.'

Blood dripped from a cut on my left hand – roof tiles were goddamn sharp. 'Your ex?' I repeated. 'How would your ex even know who I am? And why would she do this?'

His other hand rubbed the back of his neck. 'Well, we broke up just before I started in here. She didn't take it that well…' He tailed off and I stood rooted to the spot.

'And she knows who I am? How? We've never gone any-where together. We've kissed twice. How could she have seen me?' I rummaged through my bag for a hankie to stem the bleeding and came up with a crumpled McDonald's napkin.

He nodded towards the chip shop on the other side of the street. 'She works over there. That's why I was nervous last night. I mean, she never works a Tuesday, so I didn't think she'd have seen us.'

I squinted. 'You're telling me your ex did this to my car because she saw you kiss me once? That doesn't make any sense.'

He pointed to the huge tile stuck in the glass. 'Her dad's a roofer. That's a ridge tile – his garage is full of them.'

'You're kidding. You have to be kidding, right?' I begged. This could not be happening.

Dean shrugged. 'What can I say? She's possessive.'

I couldn't help but notice he seemed a little pleased about it. His eyes were flashing in a way they hadn't when we'd kissed. 'She just… loves hard, you know?'

I felt my eyebrows rising to reach the brim of my hat. 'Do I know what it's like to be a fuckin' psychotic bitch who can't take the hint? No, can't say I do.'

His head snapped around to me. 'She's not a bitch, alright? She just doesn't handle things well. Her home life is a bit mental.'

I made a show of standing next to the car and hanging over the windshield. 'Doesn't handle things well? There is a roof tile in my fucking car. Not on a roof, *in my windscreen.* So yes, this is someone who doesn't handle things well. Duh.'

'I'll speak to her, OK?' he offered, like this was a complete overreaction and what she'd done was no worse than pulling my hair in the playground. Like she hadn't actually committed a real crime. Couldn't he hear how ridiculous that sounded?

I surveyed the damage one more time – both the car and mine and Dean's now finished relationship. 'Don't bother. I'm going home.'

'I'm sorry,' he called after me.

I didn't acknowledge him and speed-walked home, already dreading the conversation and inevitable questions Dad would ask when I told him. I prayed that she hadn't tampered with the brakes after he'd just spent money to fix them.

Dean lasted three more shifts before packing it in. I did see him again though. I found out through a co-worker that he'd left to go and train as an apprentice roofer with his girlfriend's dad's company.

McDonald's covered the damage to my car, thanks to a loophole in the car park regulations. Thanks to the breakdown of the CCTV that week, I could never prove the culprit, but everyone knew who'd done it. My brakes were fine on inspection; however, I made the junior mechanic drive it a couple of times before I'd even sit in it, fearing a delayed car bomb. As a precaution, I checked under the seats for a good few weeks after that.

Three years later, I came across Dean on Myspace and found he'd gained an extra chin and a baby. With her.

How did I know it was her?

Their son's name – Ridge Walker.

Like the ridge tile I found in my windscreen.

The Hitman

Ever met someone at a party and thought, *If he could get away with it, I'd be hog-tied and seven feet under his patio slabs by morning?*

That's the first thing that came to me when my drunk friend Leanne introduced me to Big Kev. Real name: Kevin Maloney. The only larger-than-average thing about him was his pupils – black orbs that gave nothing away.

I hadn't planned on turning up to this house party – or empty, which I've explained about in an earlier story. If you still don't know what that is, go and watch Kevin Bridges describing it in his stand-up shows and you'll get the gist. My retelling of it is neither as accurate, nor as funny. But to summarise, in case you don't know who Kevin Bridges is, or you didn't read the aforementioned story, it's when your mum and dad – or the adult you live with that pays the bills – leaves you alone in the house, trusting that on their return they won't find cheese-and-onion crisps mashed into their 100%-wool living-room carpet or that your friends won't make a stair slide that causes three of the bannister spokes to snap off.

FYI, this all happened during one of my empties (I got caught after my bitch neighbour grassed me in), so now I had to depend on the naivety of other people's parents.

At my last count, Leanne had consumed at least three vodkas. I looked forward to watching that in reverse later. I always carried a spare hair tie in situations like these, because a girl never knew when their friend would drink too much and require her hair to be tucked out of harm's way.

Big Kev took it upon himself to squeeze in next to me on the leather two-seater, the colour of which could be described as a crossover between mustard and vomit. Leanne's mum loved colour – everywhere – but the couch was an assault on the eyes.

I noted that he could've taken a seat on the overstuffed sage-green monstrosity across from me, which now lay empty after its former inhabitants had snuck off to a bedroom.

Instead, our thighs squashed close together. Uncomfortable didn't even cover it. When I glanced down, I compared the size of our legs and grunted when I calculated that his were a lot smaller than mine.

Stupid dollhouse couch, I snarled under my breath.

The couch squelched as he shifted positions to face me. 'What's that?'

Damn me and my muttering. 'Nothing,' I answered politely, taking in his black attire – a stark contrast to his blonde hair and milky complexion.

'So how do you know Leanne?' he asked, bobbing his head in time to an unknown rap track emitting from the kitchen.

Jesus, and now the dreaded small talk – one of the reasons I hadn't wanted to be here. But as Leanne's best friend, it was my duty, in case someone tried to steal her mum's car or have sex in her parents' room. I'd failed to mention that if someone did have the balls to steal a car then they would likely also have the balls to run over the person attempting to stop them, i.e. me. And if people we knew were having sex, then I would not be walking into that room, no matter who it belonged to.

Nowhere in the friendship handbook did it say I had to traumatize myself on purpose or use my body as a shield against car thieves.

A search of the room confirmed Leanne had pissed off, no doubt to the kitchen for a top-up. 'I'm her best friend,' I admitted. 'You?'

He chugged back his beer and burped before answering, 'Pal of her cousin.' He wiped his mouth with the sleeve of his black hoodie. Superb.

Someone turned the song up so that I could feel the bass through the soles of my Air Max.

'This song is fuckin' epic,' Big Kev cried, tapping his frail fingers in time to the beat on his thigh. A bit too close to my thigh for my liking.

I nodded in silent agreement and hoped he wouldn't ask me any questions about rappers because I'd as much interest in them as I did in selling advertising space for newspapers. My job at that time. It wasn't for me.

My luck had taken the night off.

'Do you know what this song is about?' He turned so that he now sat facing me, crossing his legs and showing off the Doc Martens that looked three sizes bigger than they should be around his shins.

I shook my head and prayed that he'd read the blasé look on my face and move on to pastures new. Or at least a different couch.

'It's about hitmen,' he pressed, clasping his hands together under his chin.

He looked just like mine and Leanne's old chemistry teacher when he believed you were interested in the periodic table – not realising you were actually trying to distract him so he didn't remember the planned test for that period.

My cup of cranberry and vodka stared back at me. 'Cool.'

He leaned closer. 'How much would you charge to kill someone?'

I stared at him, pondering whether I was being propositioned or not. Maybe even set up in some murder-for-hire plot. I'd seen enough true-crime documentaries to know shit like this happened all the time.

'Eh, I wouldn't. Not my thing,' I answered in a loud voice, in case he happened to be wearing a wire. OK, I'd crossed into paranoid territory. This was Scotland – the FBI did not loiter outside teenage empties listening in.

My answer didn't stop the conversation dead as I'd hoped.

'I would. Someone came in here right now and handed me ten grand to kill you, I'd do it.'

See what I mean about the hog-tied-and-patio thing?

I was astonished at how fast this conversation had taken a turn, and now I couldn't walk away.

'You'd kill me for ten grand? Without knowing the circumstances. Like, what if I run a charity and adopt donkeys?'

That made him pause. 'I see your point.'

I felt like I'd just talked Hitler out of invading Poland. 'After all, you'd be going on what this other person had told you about me, right? You can't kill someone based on hearsay.'

'Correct,' he conceded.

Thank God – case closed. I prepared to stand up.

He rubbed the pubic hair on his chin. 'How about this: I wouldn't kill you, but I'd cut your arm off. Clean cut, mind. So they'd have a chance of being able to reattach it.'

My arm hair stood up. 'Did you just say you'd cut my arm off?'

His stare went blank. 'Yeah, but I'd do it in a way that meant you wouldn't bleed out. You'd survive.'

'But I'd lose my arm?' I drawled. 'For ten grand, you're cutting off one of my limbs.'

He remained poker-faced. 'Would you prefer I cut something else off?' His eyes dropped to my denim-clad legs. Sizing them up for a machete?

I recoiled. 'I'd prefer to keep all my extremities.'

I would've bet money that if I checked his pockets, I'd have found the keys to a windowless van. With a mattress and length of cord in the back.

That answer didn't dissuade him. 'If you think about it, maybe it would be better to charge twenty since keeping you alive would be riskier. I mean, you'd be able to identify me if I just hacked your arm off.'

The word *hack* kicked my legs into gear. 'That's my cue to leave.' I dropped my cup in the process, and cranberry liquid splashed onto the one white item in Leanne's house – a rug. An expensive one.

Big Kev glared at the stain seeping into the sheepskin – it looked like a slaughtered polar bear. 'God's sake, look at the state of that,' he had the cheek to exclaim.

I got over my one act of vandalism toot sweet. 'That's what your carpet would look like if you hacked my arm off, you bloody weirdo.'

People were starting to drift in from the other rooms on hearing the commotion.

He jumped up, one foot standing firm in the red puddle. 'I gave you the option of your leg,' he retorted like I was being ridiculous in forgetting that point.

From behind me, I heard Leanne squeal, 'Fuck! My mum's going to kill me.'

I wasn't in the mood to stay and hold her hair back; instead, I shoved past her. 'It's not your mum you need to worry about – it's Jason over there.'

As I grabbed my jacket off the stairs, I could hear Big Kev trying to defend himself to the onlookers.

'My name's not Jason, it's Kev.'

A year later, Leanne and I were in my bedroom after college let out. I found myself sifting through the local paper as I waited for her to finish using my curling irons.

'Christ,' she shrieked from the floor in front of the mirror, burning her hand for the fifteenth time while curling the last few tendrils around her face.

I giggled at the rage on her face and resumed flipping pages until I came to a double-page spread in the middle.

Leanne eyed me in the mirror whilst she brushed out a curl. 'What's up with you? You look like you've seen an ex.'

'Not quite,' I answered, blood rushing to my ears.

Big Kev's expressionless face filled the left-hand page. On the right, in bold, underlined letters, read the headline, 'Local man charged with carrying a machete.'

Leanne turned the curlers off and stood up to stretch her legs – she'd been on the floor for an hour doing her hair, in an attempt to stop it from going frizzy when we went out later. 'Who then?'

I turned the paper and held it up, allowing her a couple of seconds to register the face.

She stepped forward and ripped it out of my hands. 'No fucking way.'

After that night, she'd spent days hounding me that I'd got Big Kev all wrong – and her grounded in the process because of the ruined rug. Also, her cousin would never be friends with someone who'd accept payment for maiming or killing people.

My long-awaited moment of vindication had come.

'Told you he was Jason.'

She Shoots, He Scores

After Big Kev, I vowed never to engage in a conversation with someone who gave themselves a nickname. Ever.

If you approached me on a night out and introduced yourself as 'Cam' and your real name turned out to be Cameron, then I didn't want to know.

I kept that rule for all of three weeks until one night, myself and three college friends were sitting in my Saxo in a retail park. The current trend for people our age was to drive around – or cruise – retail parks, eyeing up other car inhabitants to see if you liked the look of them. If you did, then you'd pull up next to them, make small talk about their alloys or some bullshit and get the good-looking driver or his pal's number.

On occasion, there would also be drag racing. Not to be confused with the *Fast and Furious* type; more Dumb and Desperate. Its sole purpose being to impress watching girls with handbrake turn skills. I'd been driving for five years by then and never had the inclination to try one. I also didn't understand it but kept my mouth shut in order to appear knowledgeable in this small motoring community.

After one of these laughable drag races is when a souped-up orange Civic rolled up next to us, its engine dwarfed by the sound of Ludacris pumping from speakers in the boot. I continued shoving chips into my mouth while I reclined in the driver's seat. Stacey, Chloe and Lisa poked at me to sit up, but I shrugged them off. I wanted no part of any boy racers – I only drove down here at their insistence, with the added perk of the McDonald's located right in the centre of it.

Even though I didn't work there by then, I still did – in fact, still do – have a small obsession with their fries.

The three of them busied themselves looking cool – a hard thing to do in a cramped back seat and a passenger chair with only enough legroom for a garden gnome.

At Stacey's insistence – and to avoid giving her deep vein thrombosis – I pulled my seat forward and up into the correct position. I caught her giving me a snide look in the rear-view mirror, but I chose to let it go. She'd been dumped the day before by her boyfriend of six months – she didn't deserve a dead leg as well.

The Civic driver turned the engine off, and the volume from the speakers decreased. However, the tinted windows remained shut, allowing them to view us like we were prisoners in an interrogation room.

Chloe wriggled around in the back seat, straining to see through their windows. 'Aw please let them be good-looking and Italian.'

Chloe's family were all old-school Italian, which meant they wanted her to marry an Italian. I say wanted, but I got the distinct impression the few times I'd met Chloe's dad that nothing but an Italian would do. I'd made the unfortunate error of asking him why once during pre-drinks at Chloe's, and the hand gestures he'd made – plus the accompanying scowl – had taught me never to ask again. He'd been born and raised in Naples, and despite thirty years in Scotland, he still carried the thick accent, so I couldn't even tell you what he said. But it didn't come across as complimentary to us 'non-Italians'. I swore to Stacey later that night in the toilets that I'd heard the word slag. She'd poked me in the eye with a powder brush and told me I tended to overreact.

You're almost finished with this book now, so some of you may agree with that.

Lisa flipped the passenger-side visor down and reapplied her lipstick, using the headlights of the Corsa in front of us to see what she was doing. 'If you want Italian, go to Italy,' she garbled through an open mouth as she applied a second layer of Berry Kisses.

I turned in my seat to face Chloe. 'You want a dick, you come to the retail park.'

All four of us erupted in laughter, which meant we missed the sound of the window on the Civic's driver's side sliding down.

A jokey, sarcastic, 'What's so funny?' brought our mirth to a halt.

The driver had spiky black hair and a tracksuit top zipped right up to the neck. It was impossible to tell his height or weight as the car seat hung so low. The only visible part of his body was the elbow leaning on the car door, a stance most guys used at the time – alongside driving with one hand on the wheel – because they thought it made them look cool as fuck. The police who trawled the retail park looking for repeat drag-race offenders did not agree.

Nothing about my sarcasm was jokey. 'Why is it your business?'

Can you tell that by this point in my life I had no time for the opposite sex? Or even the same sex. I hated everyone.

His passenger leaned over him to address us. 'Excuse my pal – we don't bring him out that often.'

My lip curled. 'Can see why.' I'd met guys like this before, thinking they were big men because they drove a nice car. Either on tick up to their yellow eyeballs or gifted it by Mummy and Daddy.

Civic Guy did not like my tone. 'You're friendly, eh?' He retracted his elbow back into the car.

All three of my friends were whispering things for me to say, things to ask, pleading with me to be nice because Lisa apparently liked Passenger Guy's eyes. FYI, she would have to have been a bat to be able to make out any feature on his face from her vantage point. Civic Guy hadn't put on his interior lights, under the guise of appearing mysterious, and I couldn't put mine on because I was too broke to get them fixed.

'No, I'm not,' I retorted, annoyed that this fruitless exchange had interrupted my chip-eating.

Stacey rolled her window down – physically rolled it I mean. My car didn't have electric windows, so every time my passengers wanted fresh air, they had to power up their forearms. 'I know you,' she squawked. 'You went to Trinity Cross. I'm Martin's sister.'

Civic Guy nodded; he didn't look all that thrilled at being recognised. Or maybe he'd no clue who the fuck Martin was. 'That's right.'

See? He didn't ask after Martin; bet he'd never met a Martin in his life.

Stacey hit the back of my headrest in excitement. 'Um, it's David, right? Daniel?'

He didn't answer; his green eyes were flicking over Stacey, sizing her up. A few seconds of silence passed.

Passenger Guy came to the rescue again. 'How can you forget his name, man? Shady Davie? He's infamous.'

My foot twitched over the gas pedal. That kind of nickname coupled with his intense snake eyes made me want to stick the car in reverse and keep going.

Passenger Guy gestured to himself with a thumb. 'I'm Johnny.'

Lisa copied him by leaning over the gearstick and sticking an elbow in my thigh to steady herself. 'I'm Lisa, that's Chloe and this is Stacey.' I didn't point out that she'd excluded me – her way home – from her introductions.

At Lisa's request – and my convenience – I moved the car so that my passenger side lined up with the Civic's. Meaning I could tune out the conversation and watch pigeons pick at the rubbish littered around the car park. One determined pigeon held my utmost admiration for being able to peck open a polystyrene box to reveal a half-eaten hot dog.

Go, pigeon! I cheered him on in my head as he fought off his greedy pals and scoffed the whole thing himself.

If you ever find yourself wondering whether you should give up dating, just ask yourself this question: if I had a choice, would I rather talk to an actual person or watch a dirty pigeon eat someone's leftovers. That's a sure-fire way to figure out your true feelings.

The birdwatching came to an abrupt end when a blue cotton jumper obscured my view. This was followed by a one-knuckled tap on the window.

My right arm burned as I rolled down the window. 'Can I help you?'

Shady Davie bent his head down to speak through the gap I'd created. 'Just wondered what I'd done to offend someone I've never met before,' he queried.

'You haven't,' I told him, hoping that would be the end of it. I wanted to find out if the hero pigeon could defend his honour against his pals when it came to the mangled cheeseburger a few feet away.

He poked his head through the window like a giraffe reaching for leaves. 'Could've fooled me. What, you don't like my car or something?'

I drew back into my seat. 'You mean the tangerine thing you're driving? This might surprise you, but I don't care either way. Cars don't impress me.'

My insult bounced off his Teflon tracksuit. 'I get the sense that nothing impresses you.'

I motioned for him to move out the way and pointed to the opposite pavement. 'Not true. That pigeon is my new inspiration. Gets what he wants and doesn't let anyone else take it.'

He straightened up and followed the direction of my hand. 'So you don't like cars, fair enough. But flying rats? Didn't have you down for that.'

Why did this guy make my hackles rise? 'I'm not down for anything.' *Get the hint, pal.*

My friends were still in deep conversation with Johnny, who'd followed Davie's lead and left the car to lean against mine. Lisa would've slapped me if she could've heard how cheeky I was being to such a cute guy.

'I figured that as well,' Shady Davie said, keeping his head turned towards the congregation of pigeons. It annoyed me that he didn't turn to look at me.

Why do you want him to look at you? You hate men remember? I chastised myself. *Ah right. Sorry, brain, I forgot.*

'You must spend a lot of time figuring stuff out,' I fired back.

My tone made him turn back to me. 'I could spend a lot of time trying to figure out your number.' He smirked in an OMG-aren't-I-so-adorable way. 'Or you could just give me it. Your choice.'

A scoff escaped my mouth. 'Oh, I have a choice? How nice of you to allow me an option. Hmmm, what shall I choose? Give a guy who calls himself "Shady Davie" my number or not? I choose not.'

He threw a hand to his chest in mock surprise. 'What do you have against my name?'

'It contains the word shady for a start. Do you realise that word has negative connotations? It's something you don't want to be known for. And I've no interest in finding out what you get up to that makes you deserve it.'

His chest puffed. 'Just a name someone gave me at high school. Doesn't mean anything. Let me take you out and I'll prove it.'

I could hear Lisa wrapping up her conversation with Johnny, who'd now jumped back into the Civic. 'I'll leave it thanks.'

'I don't give up that easy,' he informed me, swaggering around the front of my car and shooting me one last look through the windscreen before he headed back to the Civic.

'He is so cute. You're mental for saying no,' Stacey gushed.

Davie slid into the driver's seat with the confidence of someone who knew all eyes were on him. Why did this bloody guy both irritate and intrigue me?

Davie started the Civic up, revved it for ten seconds then took off while Johnny waved in frantic abandon at us and blew a kiss to Lisa.

My hand pushed the gearstick into first. 'Shut it.' Not my best comeback.

Lisa placed a hand on my cheek. 'You're bright red. Don't tell me you like him?' she prodded.

I kept my eyes on the road for any stragglers leaving the tanning salon at the park entrance. 'No, I don't. Please don't start.'

Lisa started to speak and thought better of it. 'I gave Johnny my number. Did you see his eyelashes? Why do guys always have better eyelashes than us?'

Chloe worked on rolling her window back up. 'I would date Johnny.'

Lisa's mouth went taut. 'Back off.'

Hell hath no fury like a woman who tried to take a man Lisa had shown an interest in. Even if they'd only spoken for ten minutes.

I caught the empathetic shrug Stacey aimed at Chloe before I pulled into the right-hand lane.

'You can have Shady Davie in all his glory if you want?' I joked as a way to break the tension. Instead, the car went dead silent for an entire street.

'What?' I demanded, pausing at a pedestrian crossing. All three wore guilty expressions.

Chloe took one for the team. 'We took a vote.'

I waited until the granny crossing the road reached the other side before pressing the accelerator and continuing towards Chloe's house. 'A vote on what?'

'On whether we should give your number to Davie or not,' Lisa said, flinching. 'Johnny asked for it, because he could tell you'd say no if Davie asked.'

I slammed the left indicator on to pull into Chloe's estate.

Emboldened by the fact she could escape in about sixty seconds and leave the other two to face my wrath, Chloe piped up, 'We know you like him.'

Lisa's door flew open. 'I'll just walk from here.'

'Chloe, you have that cardigan I need for tomorrow – I'll come in and grab it,' Stacey reminded Chloe as she edged along the back seat and dived out. Safety in numbers.

'I won't forget this,' I threatened as my phone pinged.

Unknown number: *Can't believe you liked a pigeon over me x.*

Three weeks later – yes, it took me three weeks to be convinced to go on a date with him; twenty-one days of relentless texts and pigeon memes. So I expected to be blown away by this date. Amazed. Bowled over.

He picked me up in the tangerine dream and drove straight to a run-down-looking farm, signposted with a discoloured piece of wood that may have once been blue.

Clay pigeon shooting, it read in bold black letters.

Shady Davie had dressed up for the occasion – instead of a blue tracksuit, he wore a black one. With rigger boots. I'd worn jeans and suede flats, unaware we'd be visiting a mucky field filled with cow shit. A heads-up would've been nice.

A dishevelled farmer appeared from the door of the cottage we'd pulled up to, introducing himself as Joe and passing us a hi-vis vest each. I didn't get a minute to question the activity before he instructed us to follow him to the gun shed.

My attempts to avoid the dirt and puddles were futile. I consoled myself that I could soak my feet in bleach later and prayed I didn't catch Lyme disease.

After a five-minute induction, most of which I didn't hear over the wind whistling, the farmer handed Davie a gun he'd selected from one of the dozen racks in his shed.

Davie took aim like a pro, waited for the disc to whizz past and hit it with his first shot. The pieces splintered and fell thirty feet away from us. In truth, I felt more concerned about being cracked over the head by debris than a bullet.

He slipped the safety back on before punching the air. 'Yessss.'

The farmer passed me the smaller gun. 'Your turn. Ready?'

I stepped forward, lifted the gun to my shoulder and closed one eye, hoping I resembled someone who knew what the hell they were doing.

'Davie! What the fuck are you playing at?' a high-pitched voice shrieked from the other end of the field.

I spun around to see who the voice belonged to, still with the gun raised.

Whoosh! The disc flew through the air behind me.

Panicked, I made to drop the gun, pulling the trigger by mistake.

Boom! A huge hole appeared a few inches from my right foot.

A slim brunette hastened her approach, tripping over potholes and the aforementioned cow shit. 'I'm going to kill you, ya skank.'

Kill me? What made me a skank?

The farmer stood transfixed at the hole I'd created in the ground.

'Give me that bloody gun,' he yelled, pulling it out of my hands and clicking the safety on.

'Who's she?' I shouted at Davie, whose skin was now the colour of putty.

The brunette stopped five feet away. 'I'm his girlfriend, you bitch. I knew you were up to something, Davie – me and Colette followed you here.' She pointed to a white car on the horizon where I presumed Colette waited.

'Girlfriend?' I demanded to no one in particular.

Farmer Joe set my gun down to take Davie's from him. 'Show's over, folks. Time to go.'

The girlfriend spotted an opportunity and picked up my abandoned gun, brandishing it at us. 'You arsehole,' she squawked at Davie, clicking off the safety. The girl knew her way around a gun.

Davie had the common sense to hold his hands up and appeal to her better nature. 'C'mon, babe – she's just a pal.'

'Oh, you *are* an arsehole,' I responded, following his lead and holding my hands up. 'I wouldn't blame you for shooting him, by the way,' I directed to her; no chance would I let myself get shot over this guy.

She pondered my statement before pointing the gun away from me and fully towards Davie. The farmer lunged forward in an attempt to grab it from her.

I seized the moment of distraction and made a run for it through the fields. Despite my suede shoes, the cow shit and the possibility I could get shot in the back.

Another bang sounded, followed by shouts, but I kept pounding forward until I reached the metal gate, clambering over it in one move.

I landed on the other side, flinching as my paper-thin soles hit the gravel. Colette eyeballed me as I dusted myself off and speed-walked past her towards the lane that met the main road.

Thus ended my first and last experience with a gun. Did Shady Davie get shot? According to Lisa, who heard it from Johnny, the girlfriend chased Davie around the field for a good couple of minutes before the farmer tackled her to the ground.

The farmer ended up calling the police, who gave her a caution for disturbing the peace. Johnny ghosted Lisa two days later, and Davie's tangerine Civic never cruised the retail park again.

I hated to say I told you so, but what did they expect from someone called Shady Davie?

The Last First Date

Congratulations – you made it to the end of this book! Hopefully you've spent some of it laughing or maybe parts had you gagging. Spot juice, anyone?

Suffice to say, I had no hope for my future at one point, and by now, you know exactly where I'm coming from. Some dating experiences are so bad they make you think you'd rather spend your old age licking cat hair off your cardigan than take another chance.

Fortunately I did.

Take a chance, that is. Not the cat-hair thing.

I met my husband after auditioning to be a singer in his dad's wedding band. Yes, once – a long time ago – I was a singer. Record deal, music video, the lot. Again, that's a story for another book.

So strangely I knew my father-in-law Paul for six months before I met my husband. He talked about his good-looking boy. A lot. You know how parents talk up their children and then you meet them and go 'ugh', a huge part of you failing to see what the fuss is all about?

That's how I felt. It wasn't feasible that someone good-looking, with a normal family, good job and his own house wasn't a nutter deep down. Alongside being 'the nicest guy' ever with a huge heart.

Yeah, I'd heard all that before.

I smiled in the right places and kept things professional, fearing another matchmaking fiasco.

Then we performed at a local charity event featuring a few different acts, where the whole family was invited, Number One Son included.

I'd turned up in jeans and a hoodie, given that we were going to be the last ones on. The tight, sparkly, glittery dress of nightmares would be changed into at the very last minute, so it spent as little time as possible scratching every inch of my skin.

Waiting for the hall to fill, I sat at a table with my future mother-in-law, telling its occupants a story interspersed with a great deal of swearing. If I'd known how it would all turn out, I'd have brought her a cake and told delightful tales of my childhood. You live and learn.

I knew who he was when the door swung open – his dad had spent too many band rehearsals describing his tanned skin and spiky black hair for it to be anyone else.

Paul was right. He'd told me countless times his son was good-looking, and there he stood, in all his good-looking glory. He spotted his mum and headed straight for our table, stopping to chat to people on the way.

When he reached his mum's chair, he leaned down and kissed her cheek before walking around the table to greet his cousin. In one fluid movement, he slid his jacket off and onto the chair across from me. The solid build under his blue shirt confirmed Paul's stories of how long his boy would spend in the gym, pointedly adding 'since he's single and has no one to go home to'.

Don't fall into the trap, I warned myself. *He might look nice, and everyone in this room seems to know and want to talk to him, but that doesn't mean anything. Look at Ted Bundy.*

To avoid an awkward introduction – and stop myself gawking at him – I wandered over to the stage to help Paul finish setting up. When we were done, I made a point of sitting at the opposite end of the table. This felt like a trap I didn't want to fall into.

My plan worked out well as the acts started up twenty minutes later, and the music was too loud to conduct conversation with anyone. During the break, I headed to get changed, then loitered at the bar until we were called up.

In all the years I'd been on stage, my knees never shook like they did that night. Because there was nowhere to hide: I could see – and feel – him watching me.

Even after I'd walked off and changed back into my casual clothes, I caught him looking at me then looking away. Not subtle. At all.

He cornered me at our table as I stuffed my mic case into my backpack.

'Hi.' He stood in front of me with a kind smile.

My mic case fell onto the floor. 'Hi,' I answered, bending to pick it up then staring into my backpack to avoid looking at him. He made me nervous, and I didn't like being nervous.

'So you're my dad's new singer,' he stated, taking a sip from his pint glass.

His lips are completely symmetrical, I noted. 'Uh, yeah, or you could say your dad's my new band.' Instead of teasing, it sounded cheeky. I could've slapped myself.

He didn't notice – or didn't care. 'I'm Gary – just wanted to introduce myself. We'll probably be seeing each other a lot.'

Not if I can help it, my future broken heart whispered. 'Nicki. Yeah, I'll see you at the next charity thing. Probably. I better go.'

I slung my backpack over my left shoulder and extended my right hand. 'Nice meeting you.'

A muscly arm reached out, and instead of offering me a handshake, he pulled me in for a hug. My arms didn't encircle him, from both shock and that the fear of moving would break the spell. I breathed in his aftershave, savouring the scent of it.

That's enough, my head screamed. *It's a trap, remember.*

I broke away, gave him an awkward punch on the arm in lieu of a goodbye and ran for the exit.

For two weeks, I heard nothing. Then came a Facebook friend request.

I ignored it for two days before accepting. Then I took eighteen hours to respond to his first message.

Can you really blame me for being cautious at this stage? I didn't want signed up to another MLM scheme or have someone shooting at me. Running or athleticism of any kind wasn't my strong point – I'd barely made it out of that clay-pigeon-shooting date alive.

He invited me to Pizza Hut. I reasoned that no one would take a gun there. Or talk about masturbating in such a public place.

Can you tell my bar was set very low for this date? If I made it out with all my appendages and without being arrested for conspiracy to sell drugs, I could call it a win.

Due to a miscommunication, we turned up at two different Pizza Huts. I'd driven to the local one, and he'd caught the train to the one in the city centre. We'd both been patiently waiting in our respective booths for half an hour before he phoned to find out my ETA. Cut to me sprinting back to my car and driving at 90 mph to the city centre, parking in a parent-and-child space in the multi-storey and paying over the odds for a parking ticket.

Despite the late start, it blew every other date I'd had out of the water. He listened, he talked, made appropriate – and hilarious – jokes and asked probing questions without being overbearing. Oh, and he was hot. Even with melted cheese hanging from his mouth. I struggled to concentrate at various points due to the scenarios running through my mind. Mostly concerning those symmetrical lips.

What also helped massively was knowing his family beforehand. I'd spent time with his parents, in their house, building a relationship, and I knew the kind of people they were. Gary turned out to be everything they'd said – and more.

That first date made me want more. Which progressed to a third date, and then a twentieth. Then an unplanned pregnancy six weeks later.

No, I'm not kidding.

How did I know he was the right one?

Because instead of running a mile when I told him, he picked me up and swung me round with excitement, even after working a ten-hour shift and four hours of driving home from up north. His eyes watered at the baby socks I'd placed in a box; my way of telling him the news. He turned them over and over in his hands gently, just as he would the baby they were intended for. He held my hand as we told my parents, not flinching when my dad threatened to knock him out.

I'd stopped believing that a first date could be the start of the rest of my life. That it could potentially lead to something bigger: a baby, getting engaged when our daughter was ten weeks old, married a year later, and buying and selling several houses before settling in our dream home.

Our son followed six years later. Planned this time, at least.

Would I go back and endure every one of those unbearable and atrocious dates? Damn right.

Because they got me to where I was meant to be. With the person I was meant to be with.

They've also made me snort with laughter while writing this. Really loudly. I woke up my newborn several times.

Mark Twain is rumoured to have said, 'Tragedy plus time equals comedy.' Which is pretty much the theme of this book.

I bet Mark had a few bad dates in his time.

Acknowledgements

To all the beta readers who took the time to read these words and provide important feedback on each story. Also, my ARC readers who waited patiently for me to finish this book. Constructive criticism is essential for any author to improve, and you guys are worth your weight in gold.

My editor, Laura, who replied to every email (even if it was a dumb question) and always pointed me in the right direction.

Lastly, to every one of you who has bought and taken the time to read this book, despite having thousands of others to choose from. I wouldn't have blamed you for ditching this and picking up a Coleen Hoover book. I'm guilty of doing that myself. So thank you again, and please know I appreciate every page you turn.

Sign up to my newsletter

using the link or QR code below and
receive an exclusive first date story for FREE

https://BookHip.com/LTGPNZD

Instagram: @nicki__bell
Twitter: @nickibellauthor
Facebook: nickibellauthor
Email: nickibellauthor@gmail.com
Website: www.nickibell.net

I'd love to hear your feedback on *Single. Taken. Cursed.*
so please consider leaving an honest review on your
preferred review site, retailer or social media – or you
can email me directly.

About the Author

Nicki Bell is an author based just outside of Glasgow, Scotland. She is married and mum to 7-year-old Jessica and 5-month-old Blake. When she isn't playing Barbies, cleaning up spaghetti or reading Jackie Collins novels she can be found working on new book ideas. Usually in the bath to get some peace.

Single. Taken. Cursed. was inspired by the terrible encounters she endured before finding her husband, who does not feature in any of these stories. Their first date didn't end that badly, at least.

Nicki plans to release four more books in 2022 alone, if she can just find Barbie's left shoe so she can get back to writing.

Printed in Great Britain
by Amazon